THE ENERGY
OF HAPPINESS

Happy Publishing

The Energy of Happiness
Compiled and Edited by Erica Glessing

FIRST EDITION
ISBN 978-0-9895554-8-7

Cover Design by Melinda Asztalos

Interior Design & Typography by
www.BookPublishingMentor.com

Published by Happy Publishing, www.HappyPublishing.net

"Happiness seems to elude us, but it's an illusion. In the stopping of everything, the thoughts, the worrying, the trying, the seeking, well, just below that, we can find a sort of space. It feels like nothingness, peace, and bliss all at the same time. It's like there is a current that sits underneath everything, existing for anyone who wants to stop and access it. To experience that nothingness, that current that sits under everything, is happiness. Being with that current and simultaneously living life would be likened to experiencing heaven on earth."

— Cherie

"Your Dreams are Your Reality Sleeping, Wake them Up!"

— Mattie Fitch
The Dreams of Mattie Fitch by B.D. Mashack

Table of Contents

Introduction

Why I Stay Happy

As a happiness expert, and the author of the book "Happiness Quotations: Gentle Reminders of Your Preciousness," I'm often asked if I am happy all the time. No, definitely not. The next question I am asked most often is how to navigate others who are not happy, who seem to spoil our happiness. And the third question I hear a lot is "how do you truly stay so happy." Sometimes I walk into an event and it makes me laugh when people observe my happiness. It's something I am, something I be, and it's something you can be, and something you can choose.

But when people say "choose happiness" when you're going through a rough patch, well, it feels a little too simple. Just to clear things up, I am most certainly not happy all the time. I lose my temper with my kids some days, and I can forget how potent I am. I can forget my beauty.

In this book, I brought together some of the most beautiful spirits on the planet to share with you keys to happiness – and I am SO delighted with what showed up in this book! I believe you will be also. By surrounding myself with so many amazing and talented happiness experts, I became happier, instantly.

This book *The Energy of Happiness* was born from a deep desire to spur the happiness in you. To awaken the happiness you already are, and to answer the call of what you have been seeking. The vision for this book is for you to be able to open to a chapter, and find a friend in the author. My gift for you is for you to open to a chapter, and find an inspiration or a hint of how to step up your own happiness.

Here are some of my own precious insights that have guided me through this lifetime. I was born into a publishing and writing family. I am a third generation publisher, and second generation published author. I write like I breathe, and I write every day. I let the love and the light speak through me, and this is a gift that I welcome all of you to experience. Let the light in!

I found my passion publishing books written by light-bringers, and I am so on purpose with my life that I would do this work with or without any compensation. I love to help authors become themselves. Of course, compensation helps when you are living in a body that needs to eat and sleep in a bed and feed her children. So, I'm not actually giving up compensation right now but I do love publishing authors enough where if I weren't in a body with physical needs, I would still want to be helping people express themselves.

True happiness comes when you let it in.

True happiness happens all the time, so catch the feeling of it when it shows up, and revel in that.

Revel in the small happiness instances, and see if you can't share that with others. If you see a rainbow, tell at least 10 people how happy you are you saw the rainbow. When you focus on your happiness, you get to have more!!! How beautiful is that?

I am clear that the gifts inside this book are many, and your heart will feel exceptionally happy when you touch the light from the authors I am bringing to you!

Now here is an insight into the question about "how to navigate others who are not happy." You may not like the answer, it is so easy. We do want to be in harmony with those around us. So you may wish to choose to be around people who reflect joy, happiness and see the glass "full" instead of empty. Should you find yourself in the company of someone who has a lot of bummer in them, let them feel that without any judgment or need to change them. Just be in the space and let them be. It isn't about you. When you do this, and experience your own infinite happiness, you give them the gift of experiencing how to step up into your happiness, or to stay in their misery. Allow this, and you will be free.

On how do I stay so happy, I believe that this comes for me as a connection to source energy. As I tap into source energy – that is, the universal light, love and God – I am given the gift of knowing that all is well. When I feel all is well, I am able to give that gift to you, and share it with everyone I see. I love to laugh with people at the post office when it's really busy. I joke with them and suggest they process my shipment slowly so they won't have to work so hard. I laugh with people at my insurance company when I am fixing an insurance claim. I'm just funny and happy and I let people feel that bubble of joy all day, most days. I let people touch my light and I stay true to the light I am.

I invite you to step up into your light, and let others be themselves. See what makes you happy, and read every one of these chapters. Because one of the authors may touch you or connect with you in a way that few others have. Allow life to teach you things, and be nourished like the hummingbird. Ask for more, and ask bigger questions.

Be in the river of life as though and as if it is the greatest miracle you have ever, indeed, experienced.

To your happiness!

Erica

Erica Glessing
CEO, Happy Publishing
Host "The Happiness Telesummit"
Editor, "The Energy of Happiness"
www.Facebook.com/HappinessQuotations

Chapter 1

Your Golden Heart: The Most Direct Doorway to Happiness

By Sylvie Olivier

T hroughout the ages, humankind has been seeking happiness in one form or another, always
working hard and trying again, and digging
even more each time, thinking that the next experience
would be the good one! We've often been looking to
an outside source, as we were trying to fill ourselves
with happiness. We had to fill the void, feeling pro-
foundly uncomfortable due to what was lacking. We
have believed that happiness could be found somewhere and we have thought that, with some luck,
something positive would happen to us which would
finally make us happy. Until then, our life would be
unfulfilled.

I have experienced this search. I understand how it feels. Now that we have created this connection through your reading, beyond the printed words, I invite you to access the energy that is flowing, this universal energy that creates a soothing bond between the two of us. Will you take this ride with me? I invite you...yes...YOU, personally, to join me into my world, the world of Golden Heart Wisdom.

In this world, you don't have to wait or work or try anymore. The source of happiness is inside of you, waiting to emerge, bringing pure joy and enthusiasm into your life with grace and ease. Are you willing to access the most direct doorway to happiness every single day of your life? This is the gift that I received, the gift of Golden Heart Wisdom, and it is such an honor for me to share it with you, personally.

First, let me give you a glimpse of what is the Essence of Golden Heart Wisdom, so you know what you are saying yes to!

What is the Essence of Golden Heart Wisdom?

The Golden Heart is the magic gate to a sacred space inside each one of us, where everything is possible. The energetic vibrational frequency of that space is so high, it can transmute beliefs and patterns, fears, heaviness and low emotions (lead consciousness) into profound Joy, infinite Abundance and Love (Gold

Consciousness). In our Golden Heart, we shine our light with grace and with ease. We freely express Who We Are and we allow creation to manifest through us.

The Essence of Golden Heart Wisdom is to live in a total state of neutrality instead of living in a state of duality, where everything is either positive or negative. It is to allow ourselves to be taken care of, to be loved, nurtured and honored and to be given to in outstanding ways. It is to live our life in a *Welcoming Mode* instead of a *Searching – Having to make things happen Mode*. At first, it may seem unrealistic or too good to be true, but when we experience it, we really live in the realm of magic and miracles.

In ancient wisdom, alchemy was known as the science of transmutation where the alchemist was putting lead under pressure with a specific form of energy and by doing so, the metal would turn to gold.

As a modern-day alchemist, I invite you to activate your Golden Heart and access your Gold Consciousness. Today, you may feel overwhelmed by responsibilities. You may experience difficulties in your relationships or be extremely worried when it comes to your health or finances. This heaviness in your life can be transmuted. Are you open to living with grace and ease?

In your third trimester, as a fetus, you began to adapt

to the world in which you were about to live in, to survive and be loved. During the first seven years of your life, you formed an armor to protect yourself, to be loved by the environment in which you evolved and you developed your own perceptions. Your armor continued to grow over the years until it became, in some cases, as heavy as the armor of a warrior. It is now possible to free yourself from the heaviness.

Living in Lead Consciousness

This heavy warrior armor represents duality, fear, and limitations, because we are separated from Who We Are in our Essence. It involves many restrictions and it closes the door to our most secret dreams. We constantly live in the fear of being disappointed. Our lead consciousness gives power to the external world and is subject to a system of beliefs (repeated thoughts) of which we are prisoners. Lead consciousness believes in working hard to get where we want to go. It believes that negative thoughts have to be transformed into positive ones and that we need to trust and to have faith. We come to believe that this armor is who we are. We see lack everywhere and we experience pain in our physical body.

The Musical Path to Freedom

Your Essence is guiding you through the path of your

awakening. Just like in a song, you experience your life on earth playing from one frequency to another.

The Golden Heart has its own vibration, its own magical sound. It vibrates at a very high frequency in the universe. Its activation can transmute lead consciousness into Gold Consciousness, as antiquity alchemists were doing by submitting lead to immense pressure to increase its vibrational frequency and turn it into gold.

It is possible for you to connect to your Divine Essence, this double vortex of Golden Light, and let it enter the sacred space of your heart. As it swirls from the top of your head to your toes, it sparkles around you in its path. This phenomenon increases your vibrational frequency and the pressure required to completely free your body from its lead consciousness plates.

Entering Gold Consciousness

In Gold Consciousness, you are One with your Divine Essence. All you have to do is BE WHO YOU REALLY ARE and dance with the opportunities the Universe is presenting you on a golden plate. Inspiration is guiding you and you watch with amazement how few actions produce extraordinary results. Ideas and resources manifest easily in your life, as your vibratory signal emanates far in the Universe. You feel Harmony and Love everywhere, in every circumstance, in every relationship. You reveal your Light with Joy and Enchantment, in absolute Bliss and unconditional Love, as you honor your Divine Self.

In this state of being, all things and people who enter your energy field must transmute, adapt or reorganize in order to be in vibrational harmony with your energy and consciousness. The famous expression "Everything he touches turns into gold" finally makes sense because of all this light shining from your energetic field.

The Magical and Miraculous Universal Codes of Golden Heart Wisdom

When you align yourself with the wisdom of your Golden Heart and its Universal Codes, you manifest vibrant health, infinite wealth, enriching relationships and deep unconditional happiness. You live a life of pure joy, excitement, adventure and freedom. Your life is so easy!

Let me share the six Universal Codes that I play with every day. With each Universal Code, I'm offering you this gift from my Golden Heart to Yours: Your Golden Heart Minute. This is a message you can read anytime to raise your vibrational frequency in a minute or less, so you can tap into its wisdom and magic!

1. Golden Heart Essence: Gifts and Purpose

By tuning into the energy of Golden Heart Essence: Gifts and Purpose, you know yourself as the Divine Essence that you are; you share your gifts with the world with grace and ease. Automatically, your vibration rises while you watch the magic of life flowing into your experience. You are open to exponential receiving. You connect to your unique gift that the world is waiting for and you fully express it.

Golden Heart Essence is the basis of all the other Codes and this is when you allow yourself to be loved, to be honored and cherished beyond measure; beyond what you think is possible.

Take a minute to breathe and receive this gift:

Your Golden Heart Minute

Are you willing to watch the reawakening and the unfolding of your true Nature in your daily activities? This is where you know yourself as the Master of Love that you are. Let it happen!

2. Golden Heart Wealth: Abundance and Opulence

Once you are in alignment with your Divine Essence, Golden Heart Wealth: Abundance and Opulence is so easy. You know yourself as being Abundance and Opulence. You know that you are not separate, so you don't need to attract Abundance from outside of yourself; you only have to welcome it into your life.

Golden Heart Wealth is a choice and this is when your life becomes easier and easier while you allow yourself to receive and to be given to, not because you deserve it or you earned it, but for the magnificent Divine Essence that you are. You have the courage to see things collapse around you, knowing that what will come out of this experience will be beautiful, harmonious, abundant and opulent... you open yourself to exponential receiving with grace and with ease!

Take a minute to breathe and receive this gift:

Your Golden Heart Minute

Are you open to release patterns, agreements and vows concerning Abundance that keep you stuck in your track? It is more than okay to have a blast with tons of money and to live beautiful, fantastic, amazing, awesome experiences from being wealthy! Have a blast!

3. Golden Heart Cocooning: Beauty and Harmony

When you know yourself as Divine Essence and you are no longer seeking for happiness in the form of wealth outside of yourself, you are ready to jump into Golden Heart Cocooning: Beauty and Harmony. This is when you know that you are having an experience in a body on a planet. You nurture your body as a divine temple and you see Beauty everywhere.

Golden Heart Cocooning is so rich of opportunities. This is when you are willing to live a luxurious life while having a very profound spiritual experience. You see Beauty and Harmony everywhere. You acknowledge your inner Beauty and it makes your heart sing when you observe a work of art or a butterfly flying around you or when you admire the most beautiful flower. This sensation is Beauty and Harmony in Action. It is the frequency of the love inside your Golden Heart!

Take a minute to breathe and receive this gift:

Your Golden Heart Minute

Will you allow yourself to discover the magic of living a luxurious life while being very intimate with your Divine Essence? Let your magical and miraculous life manifest itself right in front of your own eyes!

4. Golden Heart Playfulness: Lightness and Laughter

Let's tap into the energy of Golden Heart Playfulness: Lightness and Laughter now! In tune with this Universal Code, you have the curiosity and lightness of a child while having the maturity of an adult. You don't take life too seriously and you bring playfulness into your everyday life.

Golden Heart Playfulness acknowledges that Lightness is who you are at the core of your Golden Heart. You are this bright light shining the Essence of your Golden Heart into the whole Universe, with grace and with ease. This is who you are! You already are doing it! You don't need to try harder or think about HOW you could do it even better! You are Lightness as gentleness, as brightness and as weightless. Lightness is an attribute of your Golden Heart.

Take a minute to breathe and receive this gift:

Your Golden Heart Minute

Are you willing to invite the expansion of Playfulness into your life? Feel it for a minute. Welcome also the energy of wonder, appreciation, joy and abundance to flow easily and exponentially into your life. They are partners!

5. Golden Heart Presence: Show up and Enjoy

At this point, you follow the guidance of your Divine Essence. You are welcoming Abundance and Opulence, you allow yourself to be taken care of with Beauty and Harmony and you are living your daily life with Lightness and Laughter. It is now time to bring Golden Heart Presence: Show up and Enjoy to your experience. You have the ability to show up to every opportunity that presents itself as you play and dance with it. Most importantly, you don't judge the experience as negative or positive. You welcome it as it is.

Golden Heart Presence enjoys every step of the way, no matter what shows up. This is when you are completely free of the influence of the outside world. At this point, it is more about YOU showing up in full authenticity with courage, while simply enjoying what is!

Take a minute to breathe and receive this gift:

Your Golden Heart Minute

Are you willing to tap into the highest frequencies available for you? Enjoy the magic of receiving all the gifts that the Universe has in store for you. The Universe is waiting for you to open the door!

6. Golden Heart Living: Ultimate Lifestyle

Golden Heart Living: Ultimate Lifestyle completes the portrait of living your life from a total state of blissful neutrality. It is when you give your big vibrational YES to the Universe! You live plenty of experiences in an exquisite elegance, with no shortcuts at all. You allow yourself to be served with the best of the best! And you assist and guide humanity with your own brilliance, in your own way!

Golden Heart Living connects you to every Universal Code exponentially. You are vibrantly alive. Through your breath, your inhales and exhales are blissful acknowledgments of your divinity! Opportunities, resources and experiences present themselves for your own enjoyment.

Take a minute to breathe and receive this gift:

Your Golden Heart Minute

Will you allow your Divine Essence to show you the highest and best way to live your Ultimate Lifestyle? Watch how Sacred Doors open spontaneously for you!

The infinity of the Universe is your cocoon and through your full awareness, you express your Divine Essence in every molecule that you are seeing and dancing with. When you receive this Divine Love through your Golden Heart, you feel it in every cell of your Being and this is when you fully and completely manifest a life filled with authentic happiness!

Can you imagine yourself living your Ultimate Lifestyle that way? This is what Golden Heart Living truly is. Experiencing this kind of vibration and awareness is your Golden Heart Ultimate Lifestyle.

When you choose to allow your Golden Heart to assist and guide you, you are changing the vibratory levels of people around you! Just by being in your presence, everyone starts to dance with their own Divinity.

Know that I hold a sacred space in my Golden Heart for YOU to live a life of true happiness!

I love you!
Namaste,
Sylvie Olivier

ABOUT THE AUTHOR: *SYLVIE OLIVIER*

Sylvie Olivier is a Master Alchemist and an Energy Expert who brings magic into people's lives by sharing with them the wisdom of the Golden Heart. Energy and alchemy have fascinated her since child-hood. She remembers being five years old and wanting to manifest an apple in her hand! She was then already living in the realm of magic and miracles.

At the age of 20, the sudden loss of her mother while she was expecting her first child caused Sylvie an extremely violent emotional shock. From that day on, she covered her feelings with a thick and heavy armor to survive and to avoid the pain. This crucial event in her life was the beginning of her own awakening. Years later, the floor collapsed under Sylvie's feet. Her husband filed for divorce to pursue his life with her best friend, who also was her sister-in-law. A couple months later, her young daughter got very ill, the doctors predicting her death if she did not quickly receive a blood transfusion. At that point, Sylvie had nothing but herself and her two daughters. She had no home, no life partner, a very sick child and no money.

This dramatic episode brought the pain she had chosen to hide back to the surface and rushed her into profound despair. She describes this period of her life as the gift that paved the way to her discovery of the immense power of the Essence of Gratitude, the pure Gratitude she came to feel in her heart. Gradually, it literally transformed her life. Her book, *Gratitude in Action–Actions of Gratitude* recounts her journey and offers tools and insights to see the light in our darkest moments. She also co-wrote the following best sellers: *The Gratitude Book Project, Ready, Aim, Captivate* and *Wounded? Survive! Thrive.*

In 2001, fascinated by the power of the energy of Gratitude, Sylvie started to inquire about the science behind the miracles she was experiencing. She really wanted to understand human energy: our thoughts, our emotions, the food we eat, the water we drink and the relationships we have. This led her to discover the emotional scale and how it was possible for her to expand from the lowest level of fear, grief, despair and powerlessness, to the highest level of Gratitude, Joy, Love and Freedom. She studied Bioenergetics for more than seven years at the Alternative Medicine College of Canada. Known as a health adviser and teacher for over ten years, Sylvie continued to learn a multitude of modalities such as quantum physics and sacred geometry, in order to enrich her practice. She's a certified practitioner of the Emotional Freedom Technique (EFT) as well as of The One Command Method and the Getting Thru Techniques (GTT) which she studied at the Awakenings Institute. She is also a Certified Dream Coach®, from the Dream University® founded by Marcia Wieder. She now integrates her training as a musician and the use of high energetic vibrational frequency essential oils into her practice.

Today, Sylvie Olivier is living in pure Joy, in harmony with her life purpose. Surrounded by her two adult daughters, she is a loving grandmother. She's been married for more than 17 years to a wonderful man who's a blessing in her life. She acknowledges how her ex-husband was a blessing too, as he played a major role in her awakening. She feels total forgiveness for the situation that set them apart. In fact, she now shares that forgiveness was not necessary because everyone involved played their perfect role. Abundance is flowing into her life and she sees Abundance everywhere in all its forms. She sees the perfection in everything, even in imperfections. She holds a sacred space of the highest order for every person to feel whole, complete and perfect as they are, while expressing their uniqueness. And she commits to serve from her highest potential of mastery, with grace and with ease, all those who interact with Golden Heart Wisdom.

Sylvie now assists people in manifesting the life of their Dreams. She teaches how to live with grace and with ease, and how to dissolve emotions and connect with our heart, even in the midst of crises. Through her signature process, she activates people's Golden Heart, the magic gate to a sacred space inside each one of us, where everything is possible. This space of high energetic vibrational frequency transmutes ancient beliefs and patterns, fears, heaviness and low emotions (lead consciousness) into profound Joy and the free expression of our Highest Self (gold consciousness).

In Gold Consciousness, our heart opens up to the Divinity of our Essence. Our body aligns with its innate intelligence. In this state of consciousness, all we have to do is simply Be Who We Really Are and dance with the opportunities presented to us by the Universe. A few inspired actions produce extraordinary results and we welcome intuitions, opportunities, resources and ideas, instead of searching for them. They manifest easily in our energy field as our vibratory signal emanates far in the Universe.

Sylvie offers different programs in groups and individually, online and offline. To learn more about her work and tap into the highest frequencies available for you, visit her website: www. goldenheartwisdom.com.

Chapter 2

The Key to Happiness Rests Inside of You

By Dr. Lisa Cooney, LMFT

For the first two decades of my life I was extremely unhappy. In my early 20s, I tried to numb out. I drank, did drugs, partied. I was overweight. I didn't care about myself. One night I almost died because of my reckless behavior.

You see, I grew up in a very violent household. I was abused sexually, physically, and emotionally, from the time I was a baby and even into my 20s.

This abuse took over my entire life. I felt guilty, help-less, and in terror all the time. Nothing I did seemed to help. Happiness was out of my reach. It seemed impossible to me to even live. The abuse had control over every aspect of my life.

Everything felt wrong, including me. I never felt like I fit in anywhere. The only thing that made me happy was alcohol and escaping: I would drink or snort anything I could get my hands on in order to not feel anything. This felt like the best way to exist: dazed and confused.

In college, I walked around campus with my eyes down and shoulders hunched. One day, the professor in my Family Violence class reached out to me and asked me if I was ok. Nobody had ever asked me this. Ever. My eyes immediately filled with tears.

This professor helped me realize that what I had been living with was treatable. She filled me with hope that I could get beyond this and create a new life for myself.

And that is what I've done. The abuse no longer has control over me. I've created a life for myself that is beyond anything I ever imagined.

I'm living my dream life: I travel for work and pleasure internationally. I recently led a retreat in Maui where we swam with the dolphins and spotted whales.

I live in a beautiful home in Marin County, California. I have intimate, nurturing and supportive relationships with friends and loved ones. I am healthy, vibrant, and strong.

I've committed the past 20 years of my life to helping others get free from the prison of abuse and create a meaningful and joyful life for themselves. I've worked with thousands of clients who rave about the results they get in working with me.

I am happy. Truly happy. I feel joyful, light, and free.

Of course there were many steps I took after that fateful day in college when my professor reached out to me. It's not like happiness came to me overnight.

I want to share some of these steps with you, along with some simple yet powerful tips that you can put into practice today in support of experiencing true happiness in your own life.

I have shared these steps with thousands of my clients. Believe me, they work. I overcame two decades of abuse and went on to create a life beyond my wildest dreams. If I can do this, you can do this too.

Whether or not you have struggled with abuse, chances are, if you're reading this book, there is something in your life that feels like a trap, a cage, some way you feel locked out of the possibility of happiness.

The good news is the key to this cage rests inside of you. I can help you find it and use it.

Step 1: Acknowledge Your Unhappiness

"Happiness is seeing all of you."

Ignoring unhappiness doesn't make it go away. In fact, ignoring it ensures that it will stick around a whole lot longer than you want it to. It's like a troublesome guest at a party: ignore it and it will create a ruckus!

You may deny you're unhappy because you're embarrassed or even ashamed to admit to others just how unhappy you are. You aren't alone in this. I was horrified to admit my unhappiness to others.

Yet when you deny your unhappiness, you're telling yourself you don't matter. This is actually a form of neglect. Really. It's another form of abuse. Imagine this part of you that feels so unhappy being left alone in a closet, in the dark. Would you do this to a little child? Then don't do this to yourself.

When you acknowledge your unhappiness, you value your experience; you value yourself. You let yourself know, "Hey, I matter." This opens up a whole new realm of possibilities for what you can be or do from here.

This also helps you begin to build a bridge between your mind and your body. Rather than leaving that unhappy part of you behind in a closet, all of you is engaged and available. This sets you up for success.

Step 2: Choose Happiness

"Happiness is choosing just for the fun of it."

In my early 20s, I didn't think life was ever going to get any better. I didn't believe I would ever be happy. I thought happiness was only available to others.

When I graduated college I knew I couldn't return to the house I grew up in. I knew that would kill me. Yet I wasn't sure what I wanted to do.

Inspired by my college professor, I decided to move to Arizona and work at a Youth Crisis Shelter. I chose to be in an environment where I knew I could make a difference.

Through the shelter, I worked with Child Protective Services to provide safe housing, education and meals for children who were removed from violent homes. I also got to counsel these children.

I wanted every child to know they were safe, loved and cared for. I wanted them to be able to lay their head on the pillow at night without any worries or fears.

Helping these children gave me happiness; as I was

an ally for them I became an ally for myself. As I gave myself the love and care I never had growing up, I discovered I could make different choices for myself.

All the ways I had been living and relating that were causing me pain? I could choose something different. I could make choices based on what I now wanted to be and do, not what I had been doing.

Rather than trying to escape (by drinking or snorting) I could choose things that felt good. This meant I could actually choose happiness.

You have a choice, too. What do you choose?

You can choose happiness by bringing something into your life that is fun, something that lights you up, that brings you happiness, just like I did.

What is this for you?

A hobby? Going to the gym? Taking a dance class? Volunteering?

What's the thing in the back of your mind that makes no sense to do yet you know would bring you happiness?

It may be something you did as a child, or it may be something you've never done before (or imagined you would do).

Whatever it is, it could be the doorway to your happiness. Choose it. Choose happiness.

Step 3: Release Your Addiction to Unhappiness

"Happiness is allowing ease."

Unfortunately, a lot of people are addicted to their unhappiness.

This sounds crazy, right? Why would someone CHOOSE unhappiness?

Well, for many reasons. It's familiar. It's a way to get attention. It's a way to connect (complaining about what's not working in life is one way this society forms relationships).

When things are not working, people take you out to coffee; they take you shopping; or they suggest a spa day.

Yet when things are going really well, some people get mad at you or wonder what drug you're on. They aren't called to support you or to take you out. In fact, others often don't know how to relate to someone's joy and success.

Unhappiness has become a habit. Pessimism pervades. Our lives are fueled by the struggle of what is not working. Yet what if you didn't need to struggle to come out of unhappiness?

Addictions are a disease. Happiness is ease. People with addictions to alcohol struggle to release their habit. Ultimately, to truly surrender their grip on the bottle they need support.

Unhappiness is an addiction, too. In order to release your grip on this disease, stop thinking you can do it all on your own. Be willing to ask for support.

Step 4: Get Support and Share Your Story

"Happiness is receiving you as a gift."

I tried to overcome my own trauma and unhappiness on my own, yet that didn't get me anywhere. I turned to drinking and drugs to numb out for awhile because I couldn't stand the pain I was in.

I finally had to admit to myself that I needed support. So I read every self-help book I could find. They gave me insights into healing and happiness, yet they weren't enough.

It was my professor at college who offered the support I needed: she provided a safe place for me to share my story. Up until this time, all my secrets and worries had been locked inside my body; neglected and abandoned.

How could I experience true happiness with parts of me locked up?

In order to stop choosing unhappiness and start choosing happiness, you need to delve into the root of your unhappiness. This requires looking at events, situations and relationships in your past. You may not realize this but your past impacts your present.

The heaviness of your unhappiness is lifted when you have the eyes and ears of a professional (like a therapist, doctor, or other practitioner). Sharing your story in this way begins to unlock you from the cage of unhappiness.

When you do this you move from enslavement to freedom; from limitation to possibility.

You can not create a new present and future until you face the stuff from your past that led you to where you are. You need to share your story, learn from it, and discover how you can create a new one.

Once you enlist the support of a trusted advisor you will feel a profound sense of relief. You no longer need to struggle on your own.

Step 5: Learn to Listen Within

"Happiness is getting quiet, listening, and doing exactly what you hear."

It may seem at odds that first I encourage you to get support and then I tell you to listen to your own guidance. Yet both are important.

Working with a therapist helped me clear away a lot of my inner 'static' so I could tune in and listen to my own inner guidance. And it's your inner guidance that is actually the key to your happiness.

Many people make the mistake of thinking they'll be happy when they have the BMW, the corporate job, the marriage to the "right person," the white-picket fence and the 2.5 kids.

Yet creating a life based on what you think you're supposed to have or based on what others have, is the ticket to unhappiness. That's because you're making decisions from the outside in, rather than from the inside out. When you take time to tune into your inner voice and allow that wisdom to guide your decisions, you begin to make different choices. You also begin creating a new relationship with yourself; one based on trust and respect. This goes a long way in cultivating happiness for yourself and with others.

Most likely you've spent most of your life listening to others' voices. So it may take some time to tune in and listen to your own inner voice.

Here's a practice you can do daily to strengthen your

ability to hear your inner voice.

Set a timer for (at least) 5 minutes. Ask yourself these questions:

• What do I want?

• What experience am I looking for?

• What will help me get that?

• Listen for and write down the answers to each one. (Don't try to "figure out" the answers just let yourself write in a stream of consciousness way without editing or stopping.)

When you listen to and act on your inner guidance, you're living from the inside out. This is your ticket to happiness.

Step 6: Weed Out and Plant New Seeds

"Happiness is allowing yourself to plant your own garden."

I'm going to be honest with you.

If you want to be happy, you need to be willing to question everything in your life. You need to be willing to change anything that's not contributing to your choice to be happy.

Being happy is an "inside job." However, the people, events, and situations you surround yourself with either add to or detract from your happiness.

How willing are you to acknowledge that something you've been doing for X years is no longer fulfilling?

(And how often do you avoid changing it?)

You can't be happy without pulling out some of the weeds that have clogged up your life. So once you've acknowledged that something isn't working for you:

• Thank it for all that it has given you.

• Release it with love and gratitude.

You can release it without conflict.

Now that you have pulled the weeds out, there is space for planting new seeds. You get to ask, "What's going to make me happy?"

Everything you've done for these steps will support you with planting new seeds of happiness.

And just like any gardener tends her plants on a regular basis, you too, need to regularly cultivate the garden of your life by weeding and tending to the new seeds you plant.

Step 7: Unleash Your Awesome

"Happiness is leaping into the unknown and knowing the net will appear."

Now it gets really good... even better than good: awesome!

As you take Steps 1 to 6, you begin to create a life for yourself beyond all your familiar reference points. There are no longer any limitations to what you can be or do. You become the creator of all new possibilities.

This is when you "Unleash Your Awesome" and leap into more happiness than you ever thought possible.

Yet you may start to doubt and question yourself, "Can I have all of this?" (Remember Step 3 and the addiction to unhappiness?)

Or you may be afraid to make the leap.

Will there be a net?

Will I fall flat on my face?

It's up to you to choose again: do you choose to believe the Universe is against you or is supporting you?

I believe in the air even though I can't see it. It's not

tangible and I can't hold it in my hand yet I can't live without it.

Take the leap, knowing that the Universe has your back and that a net will appear. You will be catapulted into the life you always dreamed possible.

The seeds you planted will blossom into more possibilities for you, too. You can't take this leap until you acknowledge you're unhappy, choose happiness, release your addiction to unhappiness, get support, listen, weed, and plant new seeds... then you're ready to unleash.

This is the recipe for happiness.

The steps have now been laid out before you, like the golden brick road.

What will you choose?

"Happiness is your divine birthright."

ABOUT THE AUTHOR: *LISA COONEY*

Dr. Lisa Cooney is a leading authority on thriving after childhood sexual abuse. As a licensed Marriage and Family Therapist, certified Access Consciousness Facilitator, Master Theta Healer and author of the upcoming books, *Kick Abuse in the Caboose: The*

Bridge to Radical Aliveness and *When Did You Become a Slave to Abuse: Getting Free in a New Way.* She has supported thousands of people over the past 20 years move beyond their abuse to create infinite possibilities for themselves and joyful lives.

Lisa experienced sexual, physical and emotional abuse herself from the time she was a baby into her early 20s. Having found the key to unlock herself from the cage of abuse, Lisa has now committed her life to revolutionizing the approach to trauma. She is known for using pragmatic tools to create quantum change.

Dr. Lisa is an internationally sought-out facilitator and speaker and previously was the host of the radio show, "The Psychology of Soul," in which she interviewed well-known thought leaders such as Byron Katie. She was also interviewed on television on the topic of how individual healing impacts the collective.

Dr. Lisa's clients come to her seeking core healing. They end up feeling safe, gotten, and powerfully guided in a deep personal transformation. Her clients not only heal from their childhood sexual abuse, they move beyond abuse to create their living dream!

Visit her site to find out more about her Beyond Abuse Revolution and to access her Free Gifts: www.DrLisaCooney.com.

Chapter 3

The DNA of Happiness!

By Cathleen O'Connor, PhD

A long time ago in a solar system far, far away a very optimistic young wizard discovered the origins of happiness. He found them in bits of star dust, the glow of a trailing comet and the magical dance of the rays of a thousand moons. Long before earth knew her first inhabitants, the wizard used his alchemy to spread the knowledge of the origins of happiness far and wide so that all that came into being from that time forward would contain the essence of his discovery. And so it is to this day – hidden within the very building blocks of life itself is the alchemical secret to happiness. And that is how the DNA of happiness came to be in your DNA!

Sitting in a darkened movie theater on a Saturday afternoon I am mesmerized by the story before me. The princess is in jeopardy, the hero prince is about

to arrive, the villainous sorceress is about to be van-
quished and our cute couple is about to live happily
ever after. Fade to black. Credits roll and I am again
back in everyday life and 'happily ever after' seems
like an impossible quest. I would be more than willing
to settle for 'happily ever now' but, since none of the
adults around me seem the least bit happy, that too
seems like an impossible dream.

For me, and perhaps for many women reading this,
happiness got all tied up with being loved and res-
cued by that handsome, fearless man. And perhaps
for many men reading this, happiness got all tied up
with being the hero protecting the vulnerable woman
and getting her undying love and adoration in return.
In real life – and you may have already noticed this
– not so much! Yet, what is common to all, across all
landscapes, all generations and all strata of society is
the deep desire for happiness. And that is because the
ability to experience happiness is part of who you are.

So, what exactly is this thing called happiness and
how do you find your way there? Well, first you have
to consider that there are two kinds of happiness. One
that is driven by outer circumstance or the actions of
others, and one that is driven by inner circumstance
or self. The deep desire for happiness that wells up
from the soul-self is the inner kind and that is the one
that most people find difficult to experience. Often the
quest for happiness is based on external markers of

success, love, acceptance, physical appearance, fulfillment and effort out in the world.

Part of the misunderstanding of this definition of happiness is the expectation that it is some sort of permanent state of being – that it should be unchanging once achieved. Yet, when the quest for happiness is driven by outer circumstances or the actions of others it lasts only for so long – until the externals change. The happiness that comes from these efforts is definitely happiness, and as long as you cultivate the ability to enjoy it fully without worrying about what the next moment will bring, then you are experiencing true happiness. And, if only that were enough, you would be content.

How often have you rated your life along some sort of least-worst scale? How often have you said to yourself, "well, it could be worse," in order to frame the level of your discontent with some aspect of your life? When you are working with externals to feed the inner fire of happiness you inevitably end up comparing yourself, your choices, and your life circumstances with those of others. It isn't motivating to have a 'less worse' situation than someone else. What is motivating is to have the knowledge and sense of personal empowerment that comes from being in charge of your own experience of happiness.

And that is precisely why having or not having something, like money, won't radically change your ability to be happy. It may reduce worry and stress if you have more than enough money, and certainly you may be happy for a while if suddenly your financial situation changes for the better, but over time you would find yourself looking for that happiness 'fix' in new places. Even love is no guarantee of happiness – sometimes the greatest growth through emotional pain comes couched in what begins as a love relationship.

When you fall in love your 'other' becomes a radiant mirror to your own light in the world. In this feeling is the experience of oneness - a merging with another that is profound, deeply nurturing and fulfilling; a beautiful experience of happiness. Yet, as two people become busy again in their lives and the wonderful mirror of your partner starts to reflect your own fears, self-judgments and the capacity you have to love yourself, the experience becomes one of duality - the deep realization of separation and perhaps even aloneness. There is no way to avoid these experiences of duality and oneness because you, like all of us, live in a plane of existence where the physical reality tells you that you are separate yet the spiritual reality (your true reality of existence) calls you to oneness again and again.

The true path to happiness is the one the wizard took – one that involves bits of star dust, the glow of comet tails and the magical dance of the rays of a thousand moons – it's one that awakens your soul-self to the memory of who you truly are and what you are made of. This deeper experience of happiness might not even be called happiness but rather contentment, purpose, joy, peace and satisfaction. It is more of a low level hum just under the flow of your life – one that you can dip in to at will. And it is activated by realizing its presence in your energetic DNA. Once you do that you find the self-replicating properties of your energetic DNA feeding the consciousness of your physical cells and transforming your experience of life.

Isn't some happiness bubbling up just thinking of each cell bursting forth with transformative bits of star dust? But how can you activate this special energetic DNA that you share with all living beings? Well, first you need to understand the components of what makes for an inner experience of happiness:

• Loving Connections

• A Meaningful Purpose

• A Deep Connection to Spirit

• A Positive Mind-Set

• A Grateful Heart

Loving Connections

Close personal relationships and love relationships (familial and romantic) are deep needs that everyone shares. Through such relationships, if healthy, you get to be understood, accepted and appreciated for who you are while doing the same for others. This kind of exchange is fulfilling on a deep heart level so making time daily for these relationships is one of the keys to experiencing happiness. Fill your life with as many loving connections as you can possibly create and your experience of happiness will produce ripples of joy throughout your world.

A Meaningful Purpose

What is it that excites you and makes you want to get up each morning and join in the grand experiment called life? In is inherent in you to want what you do to matter – to have meaning. This is another universal need that, when satisfied, contributes to an experience of happiness. And that meaningful purpose can be fulfilled in your work or through some other contribution that you make to the world around you. For one that purpose might be in raising a family; for another it might be in creating beautiful art for everyone to enjoy; for another it might be working with numbers and making sure that a business is properly managed. Meaningful purpose is found in the love and passion for what you do and in the symmetry of your talents and gifts used in service in some way – to your own family, to a business, to your community, to a cause and even to the earth and her many inhabitants.

If you don't know your purpose, then let discovering your purpose be what gets you awake and moving in the morning. Your own life is the greatest adventure possible so until you have found the purpose that fills you with passion and joy, the adventure and journey are your purpose. If you really explore all the options open to you, not only will you eventually discover your purpose, you will experience happiness along the way.

A Deep Connection to Spirit

Whatever your spiritual or religious belief system, the fact that you have one is a major component to your ability to experience happiness. Having an awareness of something larger than self brings expansive feelings of connection, joy and happiness; and allows you to be better able to put the small irritations of life aside. The energy of happiness is a soul-full energy so taking time each day to plug into your spiritual system will keep that awareness in the forefront. Start each day with a moment of mindfulness or meditation and invite in as much happiness as that day contains.

A Positive Mind-set

Optimistic people tend to be happier overall than pessimistic people. And there is no study that shows that pessimistic people are more realistic, if that's what you are thinking! Optimism can be cultivated and adopted as a way of approaching life. Optimistic people know that all experiences contain lessons and gifts and that allows them to not only move through hard times but integrate those experiences in a way that has them growing more content over time.

A positive mind-set is one that puts events in perspective in a way that de-personalizes what happens in life. Events both easy and difficult happen to everyone. Having a perspective that moves you from seeing yourself as a victim of circumstance to a person with choice of how to respond is what optimism and perspective is all about. The happiest people feel choice is available to them. While you may not choose the event, you can always choose how you respond to any event. And that ability to choose your response is one of the abilities in the energetic DNA of happiness.

A Grateful Heart

The power of gratitude is perhaps the greatest gateway to experiencing happiness. It is a deeply soulfull practice of awareness of even the most mundane aspects of life. In that awareness comes presence – that joyful experience of connection, support and love. To grow a grateful heart, keep a journal of blessings – a gratitude journal. Every day write down all the blessings in your life that day. Notice the blessings of beautiful sunshine, the blessing of a fragrant flower, the blessing of the hug of a child, the blessing of having a job to go to or the blessing of a beautifully prepared meal.

Find a way to bless every aspect of your life -- as it is today – whether or not it is everything you want it to be. Be happy where you are rather than where you think you want to be. Be happy where you are and you begin to create all that you hope for. That is part of the magic of the energy of happiness. Once you activate that inner star dust through a grateful heart, all sort of miracles begin to happen.

The real secret is that you have been the wizard all along. It is you who collected those bits of star dust, the energy of comet tails and the brilliant rays of the beams of countless moons. And it is you that has had the power all along to ignite the happiness within you. All that was ever needed was for you to remember who you truly are – to remember you are made of star and soul-light – to remember that you are here on this earth to experience the joy of your own infinite essence.

The energy of happiness is the energy of your own being. It is the rhythm of your breath, the beat of your heart and the force of your blood as it pulses through your veins and arteries. It can no more be separated from your physical self than it can be separated from your mental, emotional and spiritual selves. It is awakened with each breath you take in and shared with others with each exhalation. So make those breaths count. Hold them in awareness. Know that you have an effect that goes beyond the borders of your physical world. Be conscious of what you put out into the universe and what you allow in.

Hold your happiness sacred. It is the most precious of gifts.

May you be 'happily ever now.'

ABOUT THE AUTHOR: *CATHLEEN O'CONNOR, PH.D.*

Cathleen O'Connor, Ph.D., is a bestselling author, inspirational speaker, intuitive counselor and life/business coach who empowers women through boundaries and balance. Cathleen is author of the 2014 international best-selling book High Heels on the Hamster Wheel, has been featured in the Huffington Post, and as an expert work-life balance source in various publications. From 2011-2013 Cathleen was co-host with celebrity psychotherapist Sherry Gaba on the CBS The Sky Radio Show, A

Moment of Change. In addition to her own business, Cathleen is co-founder with Elizabeth Harper, of www.spiritualliving.com, an online metaphysical community. Her website is http://www.cathleeno-connor.com.

Chapter 4

Wide Awake

By Brigitte Bartley

The happiest and most beautiful people are those who have known defeat, known suffering, known struggle, known loss, and have found their way out of their deepest valley. These people have an appreciation, sensitivity, and an understanding of life that fills them with compassion, gentleness, and a deep loving concern. Happy people do not just happen. Happiness cannot be traveled to, owned, earned, bought or worn. It is the experience of living every minute with love, grace, gratitude and forgiveness. To be where you are celebrated, not tolerated. If the real value of YOU isn't seen or felt, it's time for a new start.

Behind the Veil

Pieces of me withered away over the years, as I became a multi-tasking machine. My actions, my words, and my life became robotic. I was on autopilot; not present, not conscious, not thinking, not being...only doing. In December 2010, my heart felt full, my eyes always filled with tears, and I felt the urge to live; something awakened within me. I was willing to do whatever it took to heal and live, for the very first time in my life.

The next several years of my life taught me about my patterns, beliefs and behaviors. I discovered myself on levels I never dreamed possible. I realized to have a breakthrough, things first had to break down. True friendships and relationships surfaced and while many others dissipated. 2011 became my monumental year for growth and change as I started to feel connected to life again!

Having a mentor became important to me. Nearly every successful and happy person in history has had someone who they could confide in and learn from when times were challenging for them. To be successful and happy, it is very important to have a mentor or a coach with more experience than you who is someone in a position in life that you desire to be in the future. A good mentor will always tell you the truth. I choose to empower myself and transform my own reality by changing my thoughts and actions when life gets stressful. By focusing on the good things, I switched from a negative attitude to a positive one. Once you decide, who you are, what you want and you are willing to put forth the effort to get there, the possibilities are endless. You may not be able to change your situation, but you can change your perspective.

I Choose Peace

Creating a peaceful environment can be obtained with small decisions. When you choose peace, and recognize that people are more important than tasks, you have adequate expectations of yourself, depending on what season of life you're in. Peace. It doesn't mean to be in a place where there is no noise, trouble or hard work. It means to be in the midst of those things and still be calm in your heart. Here are a few choices you can make to create peace in your life:

• Invest time to streamline and declutter your home (Clutter is not and never will be peaceful!)

• Trust your intuition. Within you is an 'inner voice' that makes itself known through your ideas and emotions. Trust it.

• Schedule your week and each day to create a structured day. Value your time.

• Meditate and treat yourself well. Make time to have fun, exercise and celebrate your successes, big and small.

We will not find peace at the end of our to-do list. Choosing peace over productivity means that we accept our work with contentment, we do what we can, we let go when we should, and we discover that life is about joy and service, and that we can have both! As Martin Luther King, Jr said, "Peace is not merely a distant goal that we seek, but a means by which we arrive at that goal."

See Perfection in Any Situation

"There is nothing more rare, nor more beautiful, than a woman being unapologetically herself; comfortable in her perfect imperfection. To me, that is the true essence of beauty," said Steve Maraboli. Things in the world show up based on the way we look at them. The more we look at the imperfections of the world, the more imperfections we see. The more we see things as perfect, the more the world shows us its state of perfection. One of the most difficult tasks for all of us is to turn our attention away from all the problems we see out in the external world and to focus our attention on our dreams of what we know is possible. This is not a call to hide and pretend that issues don't exist. Each of us must learn to spend less time whining about what we currently see that we don't like, and spend more of our time on the perfection we know is possible.

If we were to perform an "energy audit" on our

thoughts and actions, where might we find our energy flowing? Close the negative energy leaks and be more positive energy efficient. To have a pure, genuine happiness and to heal, we must let go and learn to separate emotionally from the events and people that no longer serve us and have violated us. The past is the past, and it does not have to own you.

Stop giving power to the people who hurt you. Forgive, release let go. Any pain you live in can be channeled into passion. You cannot release the pain when you process it. Events shape your feelings and when you hold onto to people, situations and events you continue to give life and power to the people who rejected and violated you. This pain can be channeled into passion. This is not a situation you figure out; it is a decision you make not to be a victim any more. Forgive, let go, release and move on. Deliver yourself from this pain and live in your passion.

My Thoughts Create My Reality

Have you heard people say, "Mind over matter"? The things we tell ourselves can be very powerful. A well-trained mind can overcome pain, fear, and self-doubt. A well-trained mind can also become negative and convince our bodies of physical sensations or conditions that aren't actually present. We can pick up many negative messages in our society that train our minds to believe things that aren't true. That's why it's so important to send positive messages to ourselves. Start repeating positive affirmations to yourself!

• When I walk into the room, everyone is drawn to my self-confidence and beauty.

• I AM beautiful, warm-hearted and intelligent.

• People love me and accept me for who I AM.

• I have a magnetic and dynamic personality.

• I AM easy to Love and it is easy for me to give Love.

• I AM lovable, tender and passionate.

• My magnetism and charm are noticed as soon as I walk into the room.

• I AM successful and prosper in my business.

• I AM good enough.

Self-Confidence and Self-Respect

Be at peace with your own body and know that you are beautiful! Our body needs carbohydrates, fats, and proteins to function properly each day. Give your body what it needs while honoring your hunger and fullness. Poise and confidence go further than just a pretty face. Realize that beauty is a state of mind, not a state of the body. The size of your jeans does not dictate your happiness nor does the number on the scale determine your self-worth. Again, your thoughts create your own reality.

The first minutes and hours of our day are the most important ones, because our mind is very receptive. Feed your mind with positive thoughts to effectively start a new day of positive thinking. If you start and end each day with gratitude, you will find new meaning to life. When you start focusing on all the riches in your life instead of all that you think you're still lacking, your attitude will change as well. You'll start noticing and appreciating all the little things that before went unnoticed right in front of your eyes or you just took for granted.

In an ongoing effort to create my energy of happiness, I remain open to releasing unhealthy people, thoughts and behaviors. You are a product of your environment. Our environment dictates most of our thoughts, emotions, actions, behaviors and habits – directly or indirectly. Changing your environment can be easy, yet it does take a conscious decision on your part. Your 'environment' or your 'peer group' usually consists of about five people. These are the people that you spend the majority of your time with and these are also the people that influence you the most. If you're not satisfied with your results and you would like to change where you are in life, a change in your environment may be the smartest first step to take. The expectations put on you by your peers have a huge impact on you, whether you are aware of it or not. If you hang around people who hold themselves to high standards you will do your best to meet those standards. Even if this means you have to put a higher demand on yourself. Likewise, if the people around you have a lower standard you will inevitably either lower your standards to remain comfortable around them or you will leave them.

The good thing about being around like-minded individuals is that you enjoy each other's company because you think alike on at least a number of subjects that you both consider to be important. These people won't feel exploited by you at all. They enjoy your company as much as you do theirs. And you will have a lot less trouble filtering negative influences from these people simply because they won't give you a lot of it. They may give you constructive criticism or hold you to higher standards than you are used to, but they aren't likely to crush your hopes and dreams and try to de-motivate you.

Energy Flow and Detoxing

Detox is not only physical, but also spiritual. Toxic thoughts grab hold and consume you. The deeper you let them take root inside you, the harder they will be to shake off. Identify these thoughts and reject them today; clear toxic thoughts of negativity. Our lives are full of cultural toxins, which are those things that are culturally acceptable, but hurt our souls. Cultural toxins can be found in the books we read, the magazines we read, the music we listen to, the television shows we watch, and in the movies we watch. When we allow cultural toxins into our lives, it pollutes us. The people in your life can be the most important spiritual assets or become your worst curses. Those relationships that are a curse to you are toxic. Realize the importance of surrounding yourself with the right people. "Bad company corrupts good character." The right people will build you up and lead you towards God, but if you are around the wrong people they can be very toxic. They can hurt your soul. They can hurt your relationships. They can lead you into temptation. They can drag you down. They can very easily take you away from God's best.

A Beautiful, Happy Life

Cleanse your body and cleanse your life, physically and emotionally. Release the naysayers and the dream-stealers. Fill your life with people who lift you higher, and be one of those people that lifts others higher. Do this and you will succeed. With toxic thoughts of fear, we are often paralyzed with irrational fear that something may happen. Rather than living by faith, we live by fear. These toxic fears can cripple our lives and rob us of our joy. Fear is placing your faith in the "what ifs". So much of our fears are focused on things that may not even happen, and there is no reason to fear the things that might not even happen. Just as thoughts, words can hurt you and the right words can help heal you. Toxic words are incredibly dangerous not only when they are spoken to you, but when you speak them to others. There is power in your thoughts AND words! And the power magnifies when spoken into words.

Even as you stop saying toxic words to others, you will still have to deal with toxic words being said to you. As a result, take action when others speak toxic words to you and guard your heart against them. How will you guard your heart against toxic words?

As we release people, toxic words and toxic thoughts, each of us has the right to live our dreams. I choose to live my life with strength, dignity, wisdom, compassion and vulnerability. The beauty is the journey. Be grateful for all of your circumstances. Nothing will lift your load and shine through your heart like genuine gratefulness! "Rejoice always, pray continually, give thanks in all circumstances."

1 Thes 5:16-18. You deserve love, peace and prosperity.

ABOUT THE AUTHOR: *BRIGITTE BARTLEY*

Brigitte Bartley is a successful entrepreneur, stylist, writer, creative catalyst and mother of three boys. Brigitte experienced a major life change and started her life over from nearly nothing. She found herself in a position where she needed to create income. The thought of going to a "job" didn't resonate with Brigitte, because she wanted to create her own schedule, her own office space, be her own boss and most of all, continue being a full-time mother to her three boys.

With a shift in mind-set, hiring a success coach, getting control of her emotional state, being responsible for her time in production with daily, consistent action, she is impacting people in their health and finances.

Brigitte also enjoys fitness and being in the gym along with outdoor cardio. She teaches her clients that time in the gym won't get you the results you want without the right nutrition. She coaches her clients through Nutritional Cleansing, educating people to be successful in their health, to maintain their program for at least 12 months so your fat cells can detox, die off and be replaced by new, smaller fat cells.

Brigitte is a mom who is passionate about assisting other moms create choices for themselves and their families. She is passionate about assisting women creating the life of financial and time freedom with balanced time for family and personal pursuits, to live the good life! For more : www.BrigitteBartley.com.

Chapter 5

Spark Your
Living Happiness!

By Ann Phillis

Happy, Happy, Happy! Or not? Happiness is a blessing of life force, essential to life itself. It nourishes, heals, expands, awakens. It builds, creates, stimulates, enriches.

Happiness gives that invincibility to life – the feeling everything is just wonderful, the can-do attitude, the radiant self, untroubled and amazing!
But sometimes 'happy' simply comes and goes, flits in and out of your life as if on the wings of a whim. As if it lives a life of its own, occasionally brushing with yours like distant friends on birthdays.

You deserve more! You want more. You need happiness – certainty. Not this transient, flitting in and out, happy-moment-at-a-time stuff.

You want the lasting, abiding happiness of a joy-filled life, every day!

Make friends with your happiness

So how do you make deeper friends with your happiness, so that you are in love every day?

Take the journey to that magical place where your happiness-self lives. Where your life force blesses you with that abundant joy-sparkle that totally ignites your fired-up, radiant life.

Your heart

Where you and your soul meet, and live as one. Where you and your life purpose, your joy-force, are one!

Soul is endless joy that sparkles within you. It radiates with your purpose and showers utmost love upon you and your journey. When you open to soul, infuse your life with soul, flow with your soul - you find that true, deep, and lasting happiness that glows in the flame of your heart. You are living your life-on-purpose, aligned with the divine, in the zone, fulfilling your blessing.

This is your fountain of abundance and joy, the upwelling of love and invincibility that says to life, "Amazing and awesomeness! I'm so totally blessed!" And happiness thrives!

Sheesh ... if only it were that simple!

Never Give Up!

Sometimes it's hard to get into and stay in that deep heart place where happiness abides. It can be a challenge to stay in that place where we feel one with the abundant joy of life.

We are here to learn and grow our consciousness, to become more radiant, joyful, and sparkling beings, and make our difference in the world. And as we grow, that journey of learning gives us lessons and homework that are hard!

Just like homework for school, or reports for work, or the long to-do list at home - your spiritual learning can create pressure. Truth is, we usually need that pressure to learn, to be pushed beyond our boundaries of what is familiar, to expand our capacity, awareness, knowing. To discover the deeper soul joy and life happiness that lies beyond the frameworks of our ordinary day and consciousness.

But when you're feeling this squeeze inside and out,

when things just don't seem to be aligned, when life doesn't seem to be working out and sprinkling you with joy-force... Never give up!

If you've tried the usual stress relievers, you know ... *it will be better when I have a cup of coffee / when I get my chocolate fix / when I get the kids to bed and have some peace and quiet / when I take a holiday...* But they still don't help? Go deeper.

If you have tried the big shifters, like taking a different job, leaving a broken relationship, moving to a new city; or tried the waiting game... surely a bit more time will fix it? But...You still don't feel that joy? You still don't find that fire and spark? You still feel pressured?

Go deeper.

There is Always a Reason!

There's always a reason for this pressure. A GOOD reason!

It's nagging you because it's a SOUL pressure, a pressure to bring you closer to your deep self, your deep truth. To your lasting joy, into your life-on-fire. It's squeezing you because there's something you have to do together, you and your soul.

That's the point. Your soul wants your attention!

And it's not going to message you on Facebook, text your phone, send you an email. It's not going to turn up at the door and take you to dinner for a cosy, life-purpose, expand-your-consciousness kind of chat! Uh uh ... It's just not gonna happen that way.

Fire in Your Heart

Your soul is going to stoke up that inner fire of your being, the deep life-purpose and joy-flame in your heart. Your soul spark. It is going to call you into that fire, so you burn off the baggage that simply doesn't help, that's holding you back, that's standing in the way, that's dragging you down.

This is how your soul sparks your change, inspires your growth and shines wisdom into your consciousness. This is how your soul takes you into that place where you are one with the lasting joy and love of your life-on-purpose. Where the pressure you feel releases into knowing, growing and blossoming sparkles, and it all makes sense!

It is by going into that pressure, going deeper into your heart, you find the reason your soul wants your attention. You find the reason and meaning for your life lessons, so you can grasp the learning, expand your consciousness, and move on to your joy-filled next step in life.

This is where you, the physical human being, and you the soul being, are ONE, in the soul-spark blazing in your heart.

Why Isn't My Happy Path Obvious?

This sort of deep life pressure is a step up, step out, *step bigger pressure*. A grow-your-consciousness, shine-your-light, make-your-difference push. A shove from the universe to get-the-heck on with the next step on your amazebless journey!

That's why your soul is pushing you – so you can know, do, heal, transform differently than before. So you can grow into the radiance you are to be, free of limitations, released of burdens, conscious of your gifts, and being your brilliance, aligned with the true plan of your life, and the universe!

And when it's a life-biggy like this, whether that's an up-levelling of who you are, a big shift in what you do, a big release of old limitations, a big expansion of your inner brilliance – *whatever* it is, it is uber-normal to bump into doubts, yes-buts, or just plain can't-do-it, don't-want-to-hear-it resistance.

And when our consciousness is busy messing with all this stuff? We simply, and often, miss the landmarks, the signs to the turnoff we needed to take, the stop sign ahead, the fork in the road.

Because it is change. And we don't know what it will be like when we make that change. It brings uncertainties. It can bring fear. It can make the old and familiar seem like our best buddies, even if joy is not there. These are such totally human, and normal, reactions. But they do not give the solution.

The happy way forward is to know and be conscious, because then you can choose wisely, not blindly. You can reap the benefits in your conscious being, and create change that is magnetized in the whole of who you are, body and soul. That is a happy place to be!

Transform With a Soul Solution

When it is soul pressure that is squeezing you into a new radiance and a new joy-filled way of being, you need to find the *soul solution* to getting there, so you can fully embrace the abundance of your soul's blessings.

Unfortunately, we are not taught how to listen to our soul truth, and figure out our soul-aligned solutions. We don't learn how to discern the familiar, embracing advice of our old self from the loving grace of our soul's push to evolve into our new self.

But you know that the old and familiar will just give you more old and familiar. You've already tried that, and it just isn't cutting it anymore! If joy has left, you have to find how to move on from that comfortable-but-no-longer-aligned place you've been in, and find that deep, life-loving, soul-aligned solution.

And it's not just you. There's a big wave of change around us all, a huge wave of change all around the world. The pressure to change and evolve consciousness is everywhere, and we are all called to respond. Your wave is here! It's flowing down your lifestream, and you know you've gotta catch it!

Soul Spark GPS

When you know it's time to dive in and catch your wave – remember, you aren't alone, and you don't have to dive in blind and without your swimming aids!

The time is over for letting these waves of change sweep you higgledy-piggledy down your lifestream, bobbing along while you gasp for breath and wonder where you are going, freaking out if there are rapids and waterfalls ahead.

This change is a *co-creation*, you and your soul in one, aligned purposeful flow. That's why your soul is pressuring you to be conscious. So you are conscious of the journey. So you have a vision of your route, a plan for your journey, and can be conscious of your soul's navigational nudges!

It's time to get familiar with your lifestream navigation system: your soul spark!

Soul Spark in Your Heart

Your soul spark is the point inside you where your soul ignites your inner fire. It holds your divine flame within your body, within your inner heart. While your eyes are the windows to your soul, it is your heart that is the seat of your soul, the place where your body and soul are one, where your purpose comes alive in your human life, where your personal consciousness and the divine collaborate. This is not the heart chakra, but the deep, physical-spiritual place and home of your soul within your body.

It is so important to know that it is inside there, within your being, and not feel it is only "out there" in the spiritual ethers. Because it is INSIDE this magic place in your being where you can consciously connect with it and make it real in your physical life!

Many spiritual practices focus on lifting the consciousness in vibration, going into the loving embrace of higher vibrations and higher beings – but to do that you usually leave the body behind and rise only in your inner consciousness. There's nothing wrong with this, it is very nourishing. But if you want to connect with your soul and navigate your journey with soul drive *here on Earth* – you need to come down into your body, and bring all the deep love and knowing of your soul with you into your day-to-day consciousness and actions.

Your heart space is the physical space where the living presence of your soul vibrates within your body. This is the place to be!

Your heart is part of your living, loving, physical being, as well as part of your deep, true, spiritual self. It is your place of soul sense: where you can know your soul truths and life's purpose, find answers to life's questions, and get the map to navigate life's journey. And it is right there, tangible, reachable, in your heart. What an awesome blessing it is!

Let the Living Light Take You There!

When we talk about heart, we are talking about that incredible part of your being that creates life. Your physical heart pulses blood through your being. Your soul heart enables every cell to live and create. But it also pulses light, energy and life-force. Your soul spark radiates love and the vibration of spiritual purpose and meaning through your heart, into your blood, and that also flows through your body, filling you with these blessings.

Everything that is alive has a heart, pulsing life force and love to all reaches of that living being and inspiring growth. Everything that is alive is evolving, or it would not grow and become the fullness of beautiful expression it is to be. And just as we are alive, our universe is alive, pulsing with the love and light of the universal heart, that magnificent loving heart that embraces us all.

I call this presence the One Heart, but it doesn't matter what name you use. It is the source of life and light, pulsing that love through our universe, nourishing our world, nourishing our beings with this living light. The loving, living light that stimulates growth of consciousness, awakening of heart and sharing of love everywhere.

When you open up to this living light it will take you to your heart, because it comes from heart, and returns to heart. It is the great wave that flows from the One Heart, to Earth heart, to your heart and back, flowing with love.

How Do You Flow With heart?

Let yourself immerse in this flow.

Find a quiet place where you can sit or lie down. Breathe and relax. Quieten the maybe's, could-be's, should-be's and can't-do-that chatter of your being. Let your personal space be filled with this flowing, this living light, as if you lie in a stream of love. Breathe it in and let it soothe and still the jangles and tangles in your thoughts and feelings. It is like liquid, so soft and gentle. Shimmering and pearlescent, white and pure yet with every color shining within. Like a warm embrace, so soothing and comforting.

Bring this loving tranquility into your body, your reactions, your fears and old memories. Go deeper into this blissful and nourishing peace.

Go deeper, into your heart.

Here, in your heart, in this tranquil space of living light, you can play with your soul-vision and all the possibilities for your next steps in life. Hold them up in the radiance of your soul spark and in the flow of this living, loving light, and see which ones fly, and which ones fall. Those that fly are worth paying attention to; those that fall - well, maybe it's time to lose those options. Those that seem stuck - well, time to do some transformational healing to release their brilliance, so they sparkle-up your knowing and give their gifts to you on your path forward.

Here, in your heart, is where you find your inner compass and certainty because you are guided by the living flow of your soul, full of purpose - your purpose. Aligned with the wave of your heart's and the One Heart's pulse. Here in your heart is where you find the confidence to dive into the fullness of your life flow. Where you co-create your magical change with your soul, and embrace the next steps on your true, radiant and HAPPY path!

Magic Wands and Fairy Dust

This is not magic-wand and fairy-dust territory, where happiness is sprinkled upon you by outer events and people around you. Oh, their love and blessings are awesome, but deep happiness comes from deep alignment within. Happiness sprinkles on the outside will always come and go, as you flow on your life's journey.

The secret of lasting happiness is to get into the heart consciousness that lives inside you. Get into the light of your soul spark, the loving flow of your heart, and navigate with your soul sense.

It is pure joy to embrace and live in your body on this beautiful Earth, as your soul's temple, the place of beauty from where your brilliant light shines. To live consciously in the fullness of who you are, where your cells, feelings, and thoughts build this temple of your soul every day, and you become the vibrant, humming beacon of your life-force.

Here, lives lasting happiness! Where the joy of *life-is-awesome* sparkles in every cell!

Don't wait. Spark Your Soul!

Don't wait on the banks of your life-flow until the

universe has no choice but to kick your butt and push you in.

Don't stand in the shallows, with fear or guilt or doubt pinning your feet in place while your heart yearns to flow free.

Open to the flow, immerse in the living light, and sparkle in the blazing love of your soul here, in your heart.

Get to know your soul's plan, and know that the reason you feel pressured is a good reason, with a good outcome lined up! Your soul wants nothing more for you than to grow and evolve with living, joyful, radiant light in all you do, feeling and sharing the blessing it is to be alive, immersed in the happiness of loving flow of the One Heart.

When you become this, you become love-partners with your lasting happiness every day!

You know it's the right time. It's time to take the plunge, dive into the living flow and spark up your soul to shine on your way.

Don't miss your appointment with your soul self and life's love force of happiness.

You have been called!

ABOUT THE AUTHOR: *Ann Phillis*

 Ann Phillis is an author, soul seer, angel clairvoyant and Earth lover. A passionate change-agent, global activist and spiritual mentor, she has immersed in the western esoteric heart wisdom for 35 years, and is an ordained priest in that lineage. She is totally committed to the living light of heart, the awesomeness of awakening consciousness through life's kaleidoscope of lessons, and the magic of inspiriting positive change into all we do!

Ann is unwavering in her belief that when we infuse ourselves with soul, we become an unstoppable force for good. We inspire and manifest positive change in all areas of our lives and in our world, and truly evolve to peace. Even though we are in the midst of great global transformations, and many of them deeply challenging, she holds great hope for our future because together we are this force for positive change, and we will create the sustainable, just and nourishing world we all seek.

Ann shares her love, hope and vision through www.Nourishing-Soul.me, where she offers meaningful insights, soul wisdom and practical how-to's that empower you be in the flow of angels and soul while standing strong here, in our world.

Walk your heart path.

Be nourished by your soul.

Become that united force for good, and make your difference on our beautiful Earth!

Your life is a magic alchemy of love and spirit, here in this beautiful world. Your soul is radiant within you, guiding you, and you can find it right there, in your heart! Heed your soul's call, and shine your happy brilliance into the world. Don't wait!

Blessings and hugs,
Ann

Visit Ann on www.NourishingSoul.me and download her free Start In Your Heart audio program that guides you into your heart, where you can fill yourself with your nourishing soul light every day.

Chapter 6

Charcoal in my Pocket

By Joan Banks Stutes

"I gave you the dream you never dared to ask for." The soft voice inside my head whispered the message.

A stir-fry dinner simmered in the galley of the 19-foot Irwin sail boat as it bobbed on gentle swells of Peter Bay. At anchor after a sweet day of sun and gentle breezes, we watched the setting sun paint golden ripples across the horizon. At age 55, I was newly married and on a 19-day Caribbean honeymoon after a life time of yearning for a sailing life. Life is good. All things are possible. The calm certainty surged.

Why did a Southern California gal growing up in a home crafted from two box cars dream of sailing? It was genetic!

My grandfather grew up on a Barkentine, "The Josephus," that Captain Rogers sailed from New York to San Francisco around the Horn in the 1890s. I grew up hearing wondrous sea faring tales and the points of the compass boisterously recited by Grandad, William Thurston Rogers. He also sang rather bawdy sea chanteys until my grandmother would say "Now Will, remember the child."

Heavy plates decorated with the Blue Willow Ware pattern emerged on holidays. One very long voyage included China (the Willow Ware dinner service for 12) and India (red Oriental carpets in the living room and a strange woven basket which I still have.)

My grandmother, Arvilla Maria Lunt Rogers, was raised by maiden aunts after her sea captain father came home to Bar Harbor, Maine and discovered his wife, my great grandmother, holding a six month old baby boy. Since the Captain had been gone at sea for over two years, this was a somewhat puzzling occurrence. The children were hastily dispatched to relatives. Down East sailing encompassed a passionate family history.

In 1987 when I decided to get married after 18 years of rather adventurous singlehood, I made a list with 135 paragraphs about my new life with My Perfect Mate Forever. Composed during a six-week marathon of tapping on the keyboard of my dual floppy Compaq computer while sipping brandy, the list did not include sailing. I didn't always believe in the list, but I did believe in the brandy. At times I felt like I was writing fiction. Someone who "cherished me?" Get real! I kept tapping and sipping.

When I am asked how I met my husband, Earl, I have a quick answer and a long one. The quick one sounds like this: "I went out dancing one night, danced with six guys and married one of them 14 months later." The long answer is detailed in my upcoming book which begins like this: "I made a list."

But let's begin with how I decided to get married. I had just completed a spiritual retreat with Edwene Gaines, at a resort hidden deep in the Alabama woods. I was a full-time Realtor®, and a spiritual retreat junkie when I could afford it. As a feisty prosperity teacher with a strong Texas accent, Edwene had to lead her devotees beyond sitting, with eyes closed and repeating prosperity affirmations. Her retreats included a fire walk led by a Cherokee Indian Medicine Woman. Somehow I missed knowing about the whole fire walk part of the program until after I had paid for the retreat and bought San Jose-Alabama round trip air fare tickets.

I almost canceled. Shocked, I ranted and raved to my spiritual retreat junkie friend. Me fire walk? Get real! Too weird. Too advanced. Too…something. She couldn't go with me, but she was always willing to counsel — like any good spiritual retreat junkie friend.

"You've spent the money. You don't have to do the fire walk." It still felt too challenging, and like it was secretly foisted off on me. Apparently I can decipher real estate contracts, but not spiritual junkie retreat brochures.

Oh well. I went to Alabama.

I was one of the few who walked on hot coals two times that night.

The long preparation had included happy songs, joyful chants, clear declarations. Shouts. High Fives. And then we walked.

The next morning brought happy disbelief. "Of course it was all a game of pretend," I told myself until I went to the embers. Joy and wonder embraced me as I held two bits of warm charcoal. I had really, really walked on fire. In 1987 this was not as common as it is today. In that moment I knew all things were possible. I brought the charcoal bits home. A level of happiness and comfort engulfed me, and has rarely left me since.

Just to be clear — fire walking is not a necessary part of finding a new husband, but it brought clarity to me.

The next day a long layover in Chattanooga extended

our travel time. Finally settled in my seat, I carefully crafted the sentence that had roamed across my mind during the delays

"Now that I've just done the impossible, — -and I absolutely know that all things are possible — What do I really want?"

"To get married! To be married!"

The answer whipped across my mind instantly, emblazoned like streaking lightening. Yes, to get married! I never intended to be single even one year, and here I was coming up on 20 years. I resisted. None of my many relationships had led to marriage.

While doubt lingered, the calm assurance of the charcoal moment reappeared — all things are possible. Perhaps I would try one more time to meet someone appropriate and devoted. Part of my inspiration came from admiring the compatibility of Edwene Gaines and her husband. After the fire walk, I had watched Edwene smile with delight as he washed her feet carefully, lovingly, thoroughly. Edwene made a list. He appeared. "God is good".

If she can do it, I can do it! I comfortably reassured myself. Yes, I could do it even if I was fat, over 50, and worked nights and weekends in the highly competitive field of residential real estate. This was my loud, clear, repetitive mantra, the mantra that had kept me single for so long echoed. This mantra began to recede that day. On the airplane. Coming home to San Jose with two bits of charcoal.

But why get married again after all these years? Somehow, when I wasn't looking, I had reached the AARP membership age of Senior Citizen-hood. Judging from my widowed mother's experience, new challenges lay ahead which could be best handled with a husband. Medical, physical, and financial challenges. Mom had COPD which led to emergency room trips. Two hip replacement surgeries and limited funds required her three children, neighbors and friends to leap to the rescue. While I was currently healthy and financially ok, it still felt like a good idea to find a husband on whom I could rely. I didn't want to burden friends and my two daughters.

And what about fun? Didn't retirement spell travel, fun and adventure? And wouldn't that be nicer with a reliable, kind companion? A string of "Ah Has" spiraled into the universe. Husband? Nice, reliable, kind? Get real! What planet do you live on? My CPA ex-husband had been utterly reliable about auditing my many moves which I called "creative" and he called "a sign of mental illness." Was I dreaming? Yes I was! And all things are possible! Was I really brave enough to tackle this project? The charcoal bits warmed my pocket.

So marriage it was! Yes, I made a list. A year later I went to one dance. Internet dating had not been invented yet--so we met at events. The women came for the lectures. The men came to lean on the brown paneled walls while sipping a single beer. Some women stayed to dance. Some men asked them to dance. Awkward, yes, but every so often magic happened.

I had a real estate appointment that night. It cancelled. My long suffering and generous friend, Pat, met me at the lecture-dance in Los Gatos. Earl arrived at a Saratoga event which had cancelled. He headed to Los Gatos. Was it fate? Perhaps. Divine intervention? I don't know, but there we were standing in line waiting to buy a drink. I made a remark that I considered hilariously funny. He grunted.

"What a grouch," I said to Pat. Harrumph. Onward!

Later he asked me to dance. His dancing was creative and unconventional, yet soon I was able to follow him as though joined with a cord, navel to navel. It seemed magical. Later, we were often asked if we had performed professionally.

As we danced, he confessed that he was looking for a date for a holiday party at the Monterey Peninsula Yacht Club!

Oh my God. A sailor! My heart stood still. By the third magical dance and probably a yacht club party date, I had forgotten the grouch thing. Oh, and by the way, he spent weekends crewing in races. He was kind of chunky and over 50. We both had weekend commitments. The sailing part was the secret yearning, the unspoken desire. Something so wonderful that I wouldn't dare to ask, even if I carried bits of charcoal.

Prior to the 19-day honeymoon, I had been on a sail boat for three low wind afternoons. Our first ten days were 20- to 30-knot winds, serious sailing weather. Earl loved it. I was terrified at times. However, when I had to take the wheel and drive over 12-foot swells, something came over me, and I absolutely knew how to do it. The ghost of my Master Captain Great Grandfather? I don't know, but I sailed calmly. At dinner on the tenth night, I got mad! I told God and Earl "Enough is enough!" We changed course slightly and the wind died slightly.

I discovered that sailing is 10 percent pure joy, ten per cent pure terror, and eighty percent hanging out on the boat. We lived for the moments of perfection – the wind not too tough nor too weak. Just right for pushing us along. The boat behaved, dancing while water slap-slapped the hull. The sun warmed us as we savored the joyousness of the quiet moment. Today, 24 years later, I am reading this to Earl. We both become wistful, silent, tearful.

We have shared our Senior Citizen-hood issues — including health, financial and physical. I had uterine cancer removed with a hysterectomy. Earl almost died with a urinary tract infection and blood clots. He was given six weeks to six months to live two years ago. I asked him if he cared if he fell down dead on the kitchen floor or the wharf at Santa Cruz. He said "I don't care."

"Then we are going to Santa Cruz." The Hospice people got mad. We fired them.

Financially, we lost a lot of money in the dot com bust and again in the 2008 meltdown. I became a Financial Advisor Representative and rebuilt our portfolio. Earl bought Apple stock and didn't sell it. We lost money in the real estate crash. Real estate is coming back.

We don't sail any more, it is too difficult. Two of our grandsons are taking sailing lessons this summer. We walk more slowly, but for age 79 we are in pretty good shape. I do pilates and weight lifting every week. Earl walks a mile in the park each day. I just got back from a five-day convention trip to Las Vegas. Patrick, my grandson, went with me. Earl stayed home and took care of our three kitties that we adopted last year. Who ever thought we would have three adorable, loving kitties? Cassie, my grand-daughter, and I plan to go to Paris in 2016 when she graduates from high school. Earl is going to meet me in Paris and then we plan to go to Germany for a week or so. And....

Oh – by the way, I still have the bits of charcoal.

ABOUT THE AUTHOR: *JOAN BANKS STUTES*

Joan Banks Stutes discovered manifestation principles in the early 1970s when the basic principles helped transform her life as a single Mom with two grade-school daughters. These same basic ideas secretly taught for many years are now a common part of every beginning sales training course. She used these visualization and affirmation ideas to create a comfortable income for her, Rebecca and Margery by excelling in residential real estate sales in Silicon Valley.

After 18 years of dating, partying, working, and studying, she walked on fire and decided it was time to get married. She loves helping people by sharing her story which will be detailed in an upcoming book. For now, her chapter is like a confidential chat with a trusted friend who is seeking happiness in a lasting relationship.

Joan and Earl celebrated 25 years of marriage in 2014. They are 79 and plan to travel the world again during the next 20 years.

Chapter 7

Realizing Happiness

By Megan Schapp

What I realized. When I was just about 40 years old, I was forced to grow up! Some may find that hard to believe since I was a wife, mother of three, home owner and an accomplished teacher. From the world's perspective, I was a grown up! What I realized a few days before my 40th birthday was that I did not feel like a grown up. I realized that I **was** still my mother's *only child* and looked to my mother for so many things, especially as a sounding board in most decisions I made.

My mother fell on black ice on April Fool's day as she walked into church. This accident left her paralyzed on one side. She endured months of rehabilitation, starting without any words and very little movement. She never gave up and after eighteen months reached her goal of returning home. When my mother fell, my life, my husband's, my children's and of course, my mother's life changed in the blink of an eye. I became the parent and she became the child. My husband had to take on a bigger role with the children and my children lost the grandmother than they had known. I realized that at 40, I was my own person and now officially a grown up.

At that time, I had no idea about energy. I prided myself on being a spiritual educated woman, but I had not come across the teachings of energy. As I embarked on the next seven years of my life, although I didn't know it, I was a perfect study in energy! I found inner strength that I didn't know was there; I followed my mothers' teachings and became an advocate for her, always leading with love. When professionals told me that my mother would always need 24-hour care, I told them that they did not know my mother and what she intended to do when she set her mind to it! When professionals would not walk her daily, I found non-conventional ways to help her. As a result of my mother's energy, unwavering spirit and trust in the world, she moved mountains. She never gave up and was always positive. My mother, along with the universe, made great things happen!

My mother never complained. Her drive was contagious as she learned to talk again, and to walk again, with some support and live her new life. She was happy! Her life was a true example of happiness not being circumstantial. She often sat in a room and just took everything in! She was often quietly observing life but always with a smile. After seven glorious years, as we sat in the emergency room one last time, my mother informed me that she was ready to go! "Oh, honey, it's okay, I am ready," were the kindest, most loving words a mother could say to a child at their death. During her final moments, she lifted her head when she heard my voice and waited for me to hold her hand as she took her last breath. A remarkable death for a remarkable woman! We had an incredible ride full of much joy and happiness; I would not be honest if I said there was no sorrow or frustration, but we chose to focus on the positive, on the happiness in life. The final seven years of my mother's life were a gift, for her, me, my family and anyone she came in contact with. She truly lived her life with gratitude!

After her death, I searched for my passion, finding what feeds my soul. I was led to the study of energy and life coaching. (I have always been a life coach without the training and credentials. I have lived this work without knowing the names of the tools and teachings.) The purpose of my life is to share what my mother taught me so that each and every person I touch can teach others; in my opinion, this really is the start of the ripple effect. My mother influenced me to become who I am and I hope to impact the life of others in a similar way. I realize that my mother still guides me; I feel her with me as I approach each day. She enriched my life so much and for that I am eternally grateful.

As I began my studies, I quickly learned about the Law of Attraction from a book on my mother's coffee table! This was truly a nudge from the Universe. The first thing that struck me was *like energy attracts like energy*. I started to tell everyone I came in contact with about energy. I taught my children about the magnetic power of energy. One of our favorite sayings in our house is, "You need to change your frequency in the Universe." It works! When we are in the flow, life is wonderful! When we are not in the flow, life can feel stressful, challenging, unhappy or miserable! We are magnets and we attract what we think. My mother never gave up hope; she thought positive thoughts and good things came to her.

One of my powerful memories of how good comes to you happened when I was very stressed, not sure what to do next to help my mother and really struggling with how to be in so many places at once. Out of the blue (now I would call this *synchronistic, a nudge from the Universe or a wink from an angel)*, a friend of my mother's whom I had never met, Donna, reached out to me. She loved my mother dearly and wanted to help her; she led me to several therapists at a different rehabilitation center and she agreed to drive my mother there weekly, lift her in and out of her car and then kept her company through dinner. (Remember I mentioned that we were doing things non-conventionally!) That is not the end of the story. Donna's best friend, Patricia, was looking for a job when my mother was preparing to go home. Patricia became another daughter to my mother as well as a sister to me; she truly was an earthly angel to us. The Universe provided more amazing caretakers; we never had to advertise. People literally were dropped in our laps, showing up in a variety of ways; some for short times, and others for much, much longer. A first floor condominium within one and a half miles of our house landed in my lap on Christmas Eve. The list of gifts from the Universe goes on and on; these are just a few. As I shifted my energy and focused on the goodness of the world, I found more and more to celebrate. Opportunities surrounded us; wee just had to open our eyes!

Some might argue that the last years of my mother's life were not fair but this was her journey, her life, and she cherished it. Being in a wheelchair is not ideal and certainly having health problems can be challenging. Many people like to voice their opinions about our lives; they freely share what they think we should do! Often these opinions are negative. When my mother first fell, I clearly remember a physical therapist telling me that my mother would never walk again and would need round the clock care in a nursing home!

Well, if we had embraced the physical therapist's opinion, my mother may not have progressed as much as she did. People often think and behave in negative ways; it is virtually impossible to ignore all negativity but we can try. We do not have to jump into the box of negativity that others are in. We can control ourselves and our energy; we have the power to do that, no matter what is happening around us. When someone else's vibration impacts on us, because at times, it does, we must stop and acknowledge what is happening. In order to not take on someone else's negativity, first, recognize what is happening, take a deep breath and share a positive message with yourself, such as, "I love myself. I honor myself. I choose to be positive." Repeat these or similar statements as often as necessary. You cannot have a negative and positive thought at the same time.

When around negativity, ask yourself why this situation may be happening to you, what you can learn and how you can grow from this. A little bit of discomfort is normal and appropriate. This is a process; be kind and gentle to yourself as you learn new strategies! I also teach my clients to put an *energetic* bubble up around them. Some days, I put up my energetic bubble which protects me from what others are sending out. Living with three teenagers is delightful and at times, challenging. I use this strategy when the life of the teenagers becomes *dramatic*. I am aware of what is happening and I don't take on the negativity.

We each are a *work in progress* and taking baby steps should be celebrated! Baby steps create big changes!

My mother never expected to fall and become paralyzed. She was thrown a curve ball. When life throws you a curve ball, big or small, you need a plan for how to handle the unexpected. A strategy for how to handle the unexpected is to stop and focus on the blessings in your life, showing gratitude. Being grateful for what is in your life is an easy, practical way to change your vibration quickly, especially when things are going well in your life. When life throws that curve ball, finding gratitude takes a bit more focus but is possible. There is lots of research on the benefits of being thankful. Just as you cannot have a positive and negative thought simultaneously, you cannot be in gratitude and negativity at the same time.

A daily Gratitude Journal is a place where you write things that you are grateful for. If you start your day by writing in your gratitude journal, you are at a high vibration; if you write in your journal at night, you will sleep well with these blessings swirling around you. If these times do not work for you, then find a few minutes anytime during your day. Sometimes on extra busy days, I say what I appreciate as I drive around town. I started my Gratitude Journal shortly after my mother died. It was one of the most powerful strategies for me during a difficult time in my life, especially when the sense of loss was so profound.

I still carry my journal with me wherever I go and believe me, I pull it out and write when I least expect to. I am constantly in awe of the beauty that surrounds me – the trees, the sky, the sun, and even the snow!

As is evident in my mother's life, negativity and pain happen in our lives. When we re-frame the negativity and turn it into a positive, we are changing our energetic frequency. Developing awareness is the first step to getting in the flow. When you are in the flow energetically, you shine. When you shine, people are attracted to your love and light. You can influence everyone you come in contact with. The ripple effect influences the world one person at a time. When you smile, the world is brighter. I smile and say hello to everyone I see; some people smile back and others frown! I keep smiling. Recently I was at the grocery store and it was so crowded! I kept my smile on and made positive comments to people who were nearby and I believe that I changed the energy of some shoppers! Positive energy is contagious. People rise to your vibration. They don't even know that they are doing that! The beauty of energy is that you don't even have to know what it is for it to impact your life.

Once I was uninformed and making a difference in the world; now I realize that I am more informed and was making a more conscious, positive difference in the world. Each day I choose this positive philosophy. I wish the same for you!

About the Author: Megan Schapp

Do you feel stressed and over-whelmed when you wake up in the morning? Does your heart race when you think about what you have to accomplish today? Do you take care of your family and forget to take care of you? If someone asked you about your life, would you say everything was just fine? That was Megan Gugino Schapp before she made the choice to live in the moment, enjoy life to its fullest and find the happiness in each day. Megan is a graduate of the University of Michigan where she earned a Bachelor of Arts in Psychology; she continued her formal education by earning a Master's Degree in Education. She coaches happiness! Connect with Megan at www.EverythingOnPurpose.com.

Chapter 8

Happily Ever After: Parenting in a New Paradigm

By Melinda Asztalos

What is possible, in your world, to live with more ease, more joy and more energy as a parent?

Today, so many parents seem to be at a loss as to what formula or method is the "right way" to follow so they can succeed in their parenting journey, based on their conclusions of what "good" parenting has to be. How much fear has been instilled that if you "do it wrong" your child will be messed up and you have failed.

What if you were willing to be kinder to you? What if kindness had do with stepping out of the judgments that have been imposed upon you that you decided are real and true? When you are willing to explore the energy that is behind your reactions and judgments, you begin to open up a whole new way of perceiving that can set you free.

Happy parents are not "better" parents, they are just willing to make a choice, in the moment, to follow the energy of "what is" instead of trying to force what "should be".

Children live with eyes, ears and hearts wide open and they look to parents for clues on how to live in this world. We can teach them how to survive OR we can show them how to thrive through the power of awareness. Thriving includes embracing opportunity in the form of a challenge, examining how and why we react and taking a closer look at our own belief systems and how they affect our lives. The more we take on the adventure of polishing the mirror that reflects our beliefs, perceptions and willingness to live in our integrity, the less baggage we feel compelled to carry around.

Conscious parents tend to be happier because they have gotten a glimpse behind the scenes of what triggers their heated reactions. They have learned how to communicate with their children in ways that diminish the frequency of power struggles. This leaves more room for alternative ideas, lessons in self-regulation and stronger relationships. They begin to perceive the relationship through a different lens.

As a mom, parenting educator and certified parent coach, I have had the privilege of being invited into the worlds of hundreds of parents. The one thing I have seen consistently is how much easier and happier life becomes for parents and children when there is a conscious choice to step out of judgment and conclusion and step into asking questions that create connections.

With my own child, I have seen how a simple shift in awareness and allowance could stop a meltdown in its' tracks.

I remember when my daughter was five years old, I had asked her one afternoon to finish her homework and I gave her the speech about how important school and education is. She turned to me, with hands on hips, and with all the defiance she had the courage to muster and she angrily replied: "No I will not."

I turned on my heals and stared at her and in that moment I felt myself being swept away with a thought: " Who do you think you are, I am your mother, you don't speak to me in this way."

This thought generated a feeling that pulsated with anger for being so disrespected. Before I opened my mouth, I randomly asked myself, "what is this?"

I immediately felt an awareness that this is exactly what my mother had said to me so many times before, not out of unkindness but out of frustration. I almost laughed at how precisely I remembered her reaction and I was about to "act it out" in exactly the same way.

In that moment, I decided to get really present and step into the energy of what was in front of me not, what was pushing me from the past. It took willpower and a deep breath to silence the tiger mom that wanted to be right.

I noticed a little girl who had enough. I could feel her world and see through her eyes in that single moment and I became aware that she required something else from me. I softly said to her, "It looks like you have had enough of homework. What's up?"

She relaxed and blurted out how pressured she was feeling and I could see that she did not know where to go with that. Not doing homework was not an option so I asked her, " Ok I totally get what you are saying. This is a bit much for you right now. I am sorry I did not ask you about it before. Since homework has to get done what can we do that would work for both of us? What do you think would be easier?" She laughed and said: "No homework!"

I smiled and told her how I felt when I was in school and had to do homework and then we talked about a plan that would work. We came up with a solution together without all the drama and trauma that could have taken place. I realized how nice it would have been if I was treated this way as a child. If my needs in the moment were respected and brought into consideration. I began to think of what the possibilities in my relationship with my child could be if I responded to her the way that I would have liked to be treated instead of the way I was treated.

I also noticed that when I gave up the expectation of what my child had to achieve and all the judgments I had about myself and her around that, things started to lighten up. Instead of functioning from what had to be done, we started to co-create the energy of, "What can we do now that is easier for both of us?"

From that energy a freedom emerged. We were no longer bound by beliefs of who we had to be, we started to become more fully who we truly are. This opened up the door to asking more questions and to discovering more amazing things that we are actually capable of.

When parents ask, "What is this? What are we creating here?, observation begins to surface and there is an opportunity for powerful connection to occur. This connective bond helps parents see beyond the story making of the mind and the beliefs that trap them into reactive behavior patterns.

When Maria came to me for a session she was at her

wits end. Her son Wesley was having heated melt-downs daily that were getting more and more intense. Maria tried to be calm. She tried time outs, she tried rewards, she tried everything she had read about. The more she tried the more upset, agitated and hopeless she felt.

Maria believed that Wesley was just a difficult child and that she was doing something wrong. Maria was is in such judgment of who she was being as a mom that she had locked down any awareness that may have had a chance of getting through to her. The more upset Maria became the angrier Wesley became and everyone in the house could feel the weight and dread of when the next meltdown would occur.

I asked Maria to start watching Wesley without judg-ing anything or making meaning out of anything. Just observe everything he is doing. Watch how he plays, how he speaks, how and when his energy shifts. As she became involved with observation and simply watching him as he played or responded, she set aside what she was thinking about herself and what she "should" be doing so she could get really present to what was taking place in the moment in his world. She discovered Wesley was not trying to be difficult, and that this was not about her being a bad mom. Instead there was something that he required that he did not know how to ask for.

The latest meltdown had to do with not wanting to get ready for school. Maria had all kinds of conclusions about what that was about. I invited Maria to ask Wesley, when he was in a good mood, not why he did not want to go to school but simply, "I'm noticing that you are having a hard time in the mornings, what's going on with that?"

I asked her to be mindful to keep the energy in her voice and body neutral. Children pick up on the energy we are broadcasting with words and body language as they feel this even before the last word in a sentence is spoken. Children will respond to that energy and it makes all the difference of having your child open up or shut down.

A neutral question that comes from authentic curiosity will give a child the space to feel safe enough to respond. A question that rides the wave of the frantic, "I need to know now" energy will push a child to a flight or fight response. This activates the lower brain function as the cerebral cortex or higher brain, responsible for reasoning and self-regulation, temporarily goes offline. A child in flight or flight cannot give you the logical response you are looking for.

When Maria asked her question she was now focused on discovering the need that was driving Wesley's behavior. As she put aside her need for him to be ready on time, only for a few moments, she was open to hearing what was driving his behavior. Wesley emphatically gave her a rundown of how sitting at the back of the bus was very upsetting to him. This never even occurred to Maria and now she could clearly see the "why". Together they worked out a plan and Wesley got to sit at the front of the bus. Getting ready in the morning is no longer an issue.

The more Maria began to observe her son and connect to what drives his behavior without creating judgments and conclusions about the behavior itself, she started seeing the value in asking questions to deepen the connection with Wesley. By addressing any unmet needs, the behaviors stopped and ease and joy moved back into their home.

Maria began to trust that Wesley knew what he needed. Maria's questions were now being generated with the energy of seeking what is possible to create more ease around shifting what is actually driving the behavior instead of what has to be done to stop the whining, yelling or defiance. The more she played with this the easier it was for her to release the fear that was driving her frustration and her anxiety turned to confidence.

Sometimes it is really hard for parents when they are locked into an emotional drama and they don't want their children to know how upset or uncertain they are.

Should we pretend to be confident and try to focus on being positive? Should we cover up our uncertainty?

I have a suggestion; how about practicing getting comfortable with the idea of confident uncertainty. That sounds crazy and is a complete contradiction, you might say!

When Janet called me for a session, she was deeply concerned that her daughter, Haley, was going to get caught up in the drama of the divorce that Janet was going through with Haley's father.

Janet was doing her best to hide her upset from Haley. It did not seem to be working very well. Haley became very clingy, she had frequent outbursts and she did not want to listen.

Janet believed that every time Haley asked her if she was ok, that it would be best to put on a brave face and reassure her child that everything was just fine. Haley was hearing that her mom was fine but the energy was not a match for that which left Haley confused. So now, the person Haley trusts most in the world is telling her one thing and Haley's body is telling her something else. Who does she listen to? Her awareness or the mother she loves and trusts?

Janet was upset with herself for not being able to handle her feelings or her life in the way that she would have liked and the more she internalized the more frustrated and discontented she became. Haley's clingy, needy behavior added to the frustration and she began pulling away from her daughter.

I invited Janet to start to get comfortable with uncertainty and instead of moving into being afraid of what might happen, become present with what she is creating that is working and asking how she can generate more of that.

Instead of pretending everything was ok, she accepted, in the moment, she might be lost. She recognized how she was feeling in the moment and instead of going down a path of panic and pretend, she told herself, "Ok I am not sure about this but I know I can find a way through it."

She started asking questions around what could be possible for her and Haley. She noticed her self-talk around Haley and she shifted from pretending to vulnerability and openness. When Haley asked her, Mommy are you ok: Haley responded with, " You know what, Mommy is a bit upset right now AND, I know I can find a way out." Haley responded with, " Oh mommy I know you will be ok because you are telling the truth."

Janet was shocked that Haley responded so calmly and with that awareness. Now that Haley could feel that the words matched the energy, she felt much more certain. This opened a huge door and Janet began to choose her words to reflect the situation in the moment without anxiety but with certainty and hope.

This opportunity provided Janet with the ability to step into her truth and to acknowledge her uncertainty and to move forward from there. Haley began to relax as Janet stepped into confidently trusting that she had the ability to create her reality.

With less tension, Janet began to connect with Haley by asking, "If there was one thing that you could change what would it be?" Haley told her that she would like it if her mom would spend more time with her at night before bed. Janet agreed and began asking more questions to create connections with her child. She played with asking questions that took both of them into a world of creation rather than focusing constantly on what was not working in the moment. Questions like:

If you could choose one thing you are really proud of about yourself, what would it be?

If you could be any creature on earth at any point in time what would you be? Why?

If you could create your own planet who would live on it?

What would they eat and how would they sleep?

What is the most important thing to you about friends?

What is one thing you are really curious about?

Haley began to perceive her mother's confidence in the energy that flowed between their conversations and their connection. She felt that her mother was right there for her and even when things were a bit scary or stressful, she trusted her mother's instincts as well as her own to know when something was not quite right. She knew that they would deal with it and move on.

Janet started to mindfully include her daughter in all things, where appropriate. Instead of trying to protect Haley from what she was feeling, Janet acknowledged her feelings without making them more significant than her ability to ask questions and create change. Life started to flow with more ease and grace and the connection between Janet and Haley shifted from fear to awareness.

Raising children has a tendency to unlock all of the places where parents need to heal and expand in awareness. Sometimes the act of looking within creates a disturbance within us. It requires us to be authentic about our own in authenticity and to take responsibility for the impact of that. Asking questions makes awareness possible.

I have spent a great deal of my life looking within. It is only when I have begun to turn my beliefs into a living reality in my life have I noticed the miracles of synchronicity show up. Looking within is not a "one time deal"; it is a daily practice that demands conscious presence. This practice also requires us to ask ourselves:

What do I value and appreciate about myself in this moment?

What am I identifying with?

Am I speaking my truth?

What am I grateful for today?

Is my heart leading the way?

What is being revealed to me about myself in this moment of resistance?

What am I willing to let go of?

What is the value of what I am creating in this moment?

When I really connect with my child from a heart-centered place what do I notice about her?

As we answer these questions, we step outside of just being someone who oscillates between celebrating and criticizing who we are and we start to create mindfully. In this way, we can uncover new truths about ourselves. When we just notice these truths without judging them we can start to choose how we would like to create ourselves. We are not compensating for the wrongness, instead we are celebrating the rightness that we forgot we were capable of. No matter what you have done or what is in front of you, you can always choose, and choice always begins with a question.

ABOUT THE AUTHOR: *MELINDA ASZTALOS*

Melinda Asztalos is a Parenting Expert, Certified Parent Coach, Speaker, Author and founder of Just Ask Melinda and The How To Parenting Club. Melinda supports and guides parents to have transformational breakthroughs no matter what their parenting challenge may be.

As a certified coach and cancer survivor, Melinda speaks to the heart of what keeps people up at night from a platform of experience and compassion.

Chapter 9

Choosing to Live Life Full On... With Bold Passion

By Heidi Reagan

We often impact people's lives without ever even knowing. As I prepared for our yearly trek with my seven dear friends, *The Adventure Girls*, a curious Facebook message landed in my inbox from a woman I met only once almost four years prior. The message read:

Hello Heidi, I lost my boyfriend Aaron this week. He died suddenly and several of your updates here have oddly screamed out about him. Your Anaïs Nin quote, he introduced me to her writing and your status about listening to your body, it all correlates to him. Thank you for shar-

ing, it's making a difference for me right now. I know we haven't been in touch, but wanted you know that you've helped me. Have a safe trip. I know people come into our lives for a reason and we're connected for reasons unknown. My boyfriend and I were always laughing together. Please send your laughter up to the heavens for him, it would mean the world to me.

> *"Each friend represents a world in us, a world possibly not born until they arrive, and it is only by this meeting that a new world is born."*
> *— Anaïs Nin*

As I packed for this year's trip, Carolyn's words echoed in my head. I remember our meeting, and though brief, her beautiful message touched my heart in several ways. I could feel her pain cascading off the page and her loss brought with it another sting of reality. My year had been riddled with dating mishaps and failed romantic dalliances as I pointedly set out to expand the experience of love with specific focus on finding a life partner. The awareness that even when we are gifted with our true love, at any point they can be snatched from our experience, was not one I wanted to entertain. Most of my life I had a recurring theme. Like many people, if I had money, I would be happy. Or, the most recent; if only I could find the love of my life, I would be happy. This Facebook message, while certainly a compliment, threatened to challenge my most recent 'if only' belief. So for now, I chose not think about losing a man I didn't even have and re-focus on the packing at hand.

There were so many components needed for this year's adventure, a hike into the Grand Canyon. It was November so all weather conditions and possibilities had to be taken into account. As I concentrated on packing the extensive list the ladies provided months earlier, I realized I was not prepared for the experience ahead. Waterproof gaiters, trekking poles, headlamp, baggies with an individual supply of toilet paper, crampons... Oh My! Since the trip a year earlier to Pikes Peak in Colorado Springs, CO, the women had been driving the point home that we must train and prepare for this trek! After all it would be difficult, it would be challenging, it could be treacherous! Every week as I counted down in my mind, "45 weeks left, I better get busy...32 weeks left – I better begin training...21 weeks left – oh dear, not much time... and so on, until, here I was packing and ill-prepared for the physical and mental challenge coming. My focus had been elsewhere for the preceding 12 months, after all, I was searching the globe for my soulmate, my twin flame, my other half! But my quests for the One left me short of the brass ring every time and now I had no choice but to temporarily suspend my search and focus on the next challenge, one that would certainly be a challenge.

You may be imagining that as a member of an

"Adventure Girls Club" I am an über fit, buff xena type woman. And while that might have been somewhat accurate 30 years ago in my Aikido martial arts phase of life, it is far from the case now. Here I was, 54 years old, out of shape and agreeing to expand my horizons by hiking 9.9 miles and descending 4380 feet into the Grand Canyon. Wait, whose idea was this anyway? As a life coach with a message that hinges on expanding life experience and embracing every moment, you would think it was mine!

The inspiration for our yearly outdoor experiences began with our group leader Cathy, and her "bucket list". Many years earlier Cathy and another friend sat down and together brainstormed a comprehensive list of all the trips and personal accomplishments they would like to put a check mark next to over the next 10 plus years. From that original creation came the yearly odyssey and the birth of the Adventure Girls Club.

This particular group of women all brought something unique to the mix. With ages varying from 52 to 67, each contributed a different life philosophy, background and current purpose, with one consistent thread. These women were always willing to venture into the unknown, push the envelope of their personal experiences, live with bold passion and laugh at themselves and each other throughout the entire process. In fact laughter and reminiscing about previous trips was often the catalyst for planning the next trip. However, on this particular morning laughter was eluding several of us as the reality of the harsh weather conditions and the challenge ahead settled in bringing the question to mind once again, "Whose idea was this, anyway?"

As we took our first steps onto the Bright Angel Trail the breathtaking panorama brought to my awareness the ongoing concern that I may have taken on more than I could really accomplish. The other women lived in close proximity to one another so while their "training" was less than thorough; they had routinely gathered together hiking the nearby mountain in preparation. I, on the other hand, left to my own devices and living five hours north of my peers, fell far short of all proposed exercise objectives leaving me starring into the abyss of the canyon in astonishment and feeling a bit of fear around the journey ahead. But in true adventure girl spirit and admittedly some pride, I chose to focus on the task at hand.

From the stunning expanse of the horizon, to the treacherous slope of the muddy, slippery path under foot, it seemed the best option was to be mindful of the here and now. We traveled the first 2 miles walking carefully and stopping briefly to capture the random Kokopelli pose with our phones (the only good use for them in the canyon). Prior to heading out we were repeatedly warned to allow ten full hours to complete the hike and with the sun due to set at 5:45 pm there was little room for unexpected circumstances. As more and more people passed us hiking up we were encouraged that we could reach the bottom in the timeframe allowed. But as our group reached the 3 ½ mile rest house and stopped for the 5th time, my concern mounted about reaching the camp by dusk. As the ladies stopped and seemed to be settling in for an extended bite of lunch . . . the words from Carolyn's FB message resurfaced about listening to your body and my body was telling me to keep on keeping on.

Against the pleas and ignoring the confused expressions of the women, I set off on my own convinced that if I stopped now there was a good chance I would have difficulty starting again, or I would hold the women up later down the road or even worse. . . not make it to Phantom Ranch at all! So, not completely convinced that leaving the group was the right decision, off I went.   I knew they would be fine, they had each other, but was ditching them the wisest decision for me? Based solely on how my body was feeling, it seemed to be so onward I moved refusing to stop for anything until the next rest area 4.9 miles away. Initially the decision to hike alone was slightly intimidating but as the temperatures mellowed and the path became easier to navigate my focus was less about personal safety and more about observing the magnificence surrounding me. I began to accept the satisfying thought that I would reach Phantom Ranch at the projected time, not much worse for the wear and with that concern mollified I relaxed and became present in a new way.

Conversation with the women was always lively and humorous, however, journeying alone allowed for a new experience and one I didn't anticipate. Challenging myself physically and enjoying good company were two of the reasons I chose to make the trip, but in the silence of the landscape a new gift was bestowed, the opportunity to listen more closely to my inner dialogue. I have been meditating for years and while this hike delivered an experience similar to meditating, rather than quieting my mind I began to take note of what thoughts were permeating my mind. Dancing around were all the ideas about not being physically ready, the judgments of myself for leaving the group and then came beliefs about myself and the failed relationship attempts of the past year. Here in the Grand Canyon, there was nothing to distract me from…well…me! The temptation was to beat myself up about it all, criticizing the seeming lack of movement forward that I had intended for my life over the year. The irony was almost too much, I was now in a physical situation were moving forward was the only choice and I was doing it rather effectively.

Relaxing into appreciation of my life and the experience of the day brought a sense of calm and contentment that had been previously elusive. I could feel my attitude shifting away from self-criticism to one of self-respect and love and it must have showed. Unlike Cathy, our group leader who will strike up a conversation with well, a rock, I am more the, smile nicely and deliver a brief "good morning" when passing new people. But with this change in personal perspective, passing greetings often turned into brief conversations with people on the path. Strangers from around the world seemed compelled to stop to share their personal revelations about their experience. From the young fit Italian gelato maker to the man running down and back out in the same day, chat after chat brought with it heart rendering tales of personal achievements and successes.

The last two miles to the camp, while flat, were mentally grueling. By now there were no passing people to socialize with and my body was screaming at me to stop. With each step I had to convince myself the camp was just around the corner, only a few more steps. It's a very good thing I did not have the knowledge that from time I reached the Colorado River I still had 1.9 miles to travel. Stumbling into the ranch I was overcome with emotion. I felt utter fatigue throughout my body as the realization of what I had accomplished became apparent. Flopping onto my cot in the bunkhouse, Carolyn's FB message once again came crashing into my mind and I remembered I had one more thing to do before completely falling out. After the women shuffled in we gathered outside at dusk to share tales, (the women anointed me the

social butterfly of Bright Angel trail), laugh, and hang
the prayer flags that accompany us on each trek. The last
picture of the day was for Carolyn with a sign I had created the night before that said, "Sending joy and laughter
to Aaron". This was precisely the moment to remember
and acknowledge the fleeting beauty of life and celebrate
the interesting people that cross our paths on the journey.

As we spent our one rest day recovering and preparing
for what was sure to be the arduous trip back out, we
passed the time meeting new people, sharing our stories
and tending to blisters. Some were ambitious and went
for a short hike to stay limber while others went to the
river to chat with the occasional rafting expedition crews
that stopped at the beach. Since it had taken 10+ hours to
hike in, as we were warned, we were sure it would take
even longer to ascend the canyon. It was agreed, in no
uncertain terms, that we would be packed and ready to
leave no later than 6 a.m., immediately after breakfast.

The first breakfast seating was at 5:30 a.m. and we were
there and ready to eat. However, not so ready to head
out promptly at 6 a.m. as previously planned. As 6:20
a.m. approached and I watched the ladies nonchalantly
pack, apply makeup (sigh) and do whatever it is they
were doing, I was getting antsy. Painfully clear was the
understanding that climbing out was certainly going to
be tougher and take even longer than descending, but it
didn't seem to be of concern to any of the other adventure
girls! So once again, I chose to head off on my own, in

the dark, headlamp in place and flashlight in hand. By the time I hit the river two miles from camp, the sun was coming up and I had connected with a group of four. The two couples were very happy to have a new person to socialize with so we spent the next three miles sharing life stories, taking pictures of the views, each other and stopping at Indian Garden, the halfway point, to brew some coffee before the most difficult 4.9 miles began.

That last bit was exactly as expected… torturous, difficult, exhausting, and altogether satisfying. People I met at camp who were younger and in better shape would pass me, but each one would stop briefly to offer encouragement and praise. It was as if were all part of exclusive club bonded by this incredible physical challenge and our sense of spirit. I felt supported and celebrated every step of the way and I did the same for others I passed.

Whatever had or hadn't happened in my personal life over the year, this trip put it all in perspective. You had no choice but to be fully present every moment as you focused on your breath and each step. A newly acquired sense of self-acknowledgment came from this particular journey of expansion which clarified my unique strengths and abilities.

The year 2014 began with a renewed sense of joy, focus, and personal growth. Living fully with the intention of being completely present in each and every moment has brought more delicious opportunities and synchronicities including a new love interest. Life is meant to be lived from a place of wonder and joy. The journey into the unknown can be frightening if we focus on that, or it can bring a new feeling of exhilaration. Make a conscious choice to live with bold passion and choose expansion in every moment, the journey is so much sweeter.

ABOUT THE AUTHOR: *HEIDI REAGAN*

 HEIDI REAGAN holds the space for your inherent creativity to emerge. A transformational leader, Heidi is able to see your personal illumination and help you shift into who you already are (and always have been). It doesn't matter if you may have overlooked or forgotten your inner powers. It is within this chaos of uncertainty, self-doubt, confusion and even despair that the creative forces of change reside. Heidi is the Insightful Muse with pragmatic tools, fine-honed over ten years of practice, research, and development that you can use to guide and change your own destiny.

As co-founder of Wake Up Women and a bestselling author, Heidi took her collection of women's short stories to top 10

status on www.BarnesandNoble.com in 2006. She also wrote a story for the best selling team-authored book for women titled, *A Juicy Joyful Life*.

Heidi is known as the Life Expansion Enthusiast. She travels the globe living her Bold Passion and working with people to assist them in expanding into the larger than life possibilities that await them! Heidi lives her life "full on" and shows others how to do the same. To learn more about Heidi and living from the Passion Zone of Life visit: www.BoldPassion.com.

Chapter 10

A Happiness Mnemonic: Real Happiness Lives Close to the Great House Called Awareness

By Sarah A. Ouellette, Esq.

There are two energy categories present at all times: LOVE energy and FEAR energy. I teach, and understand, these two energies as families that can never marry. These energies are separate, distinct and can never occur at the same time. We, as divine beings, (spirits within a physical body) are privileged with the ability to choose which energy to value and honor, each breath-taking moment of our precious lives.

I am an attorney – I graduated from law school and

passed the Connecticut bar exam in 2007. When an attorney joins the legal profession, they have the option to choose among various titles, all expressing one's beliefs, or values, on how such titles will be displayed to the public. These titles include: Attorney, Attorney-at-Law, Esquire, Lawyer or Counselor-at-law. For the longest time I disliked being called Attorney Ouellette. I'd quickly invite clients to address me as Sarah. As I've embraced my own unique way of sharing my education, experience and understanding of the legal profession, I've chosen to identify myself as a "holistic counselor-at-law." The idea being that I believe our laws have limitations by their nature and design. Their essence is FEAR energy. I chose to counsel my clients towards solutions using the law as one of many options, rather than a guide or the only path to resolution.

Laws are human-made: and therefore, are part of the physical. I've experienced first-hand my body's limits when my spirit is ready to soar. Sometimes, it's hard for the body to catch up to the spirit. When on the verge of greatness the body may breakdown, get sick or get hurt, which is why I believe the law is like the physical body: it has its limits. For example, in my family law practice, litigants who may have the best intentions, sometimes get stalled, stopped, or beaten by FEAR energy. When a person makes choices based on limitations rather than truth and alignment their spirit remain stuck in FEAR. Embracing truth and divinity and living ones' lives according to our integrity rather than physical laws or others code, enables a person to expand and flourish in limitless ways. Such decision creates LOVE energy, allowing for happiness energy to unfold.

You might find it odd that an attorney has a chapter in a book entitled *The Energy of Happiness*. Maybe that is because the legal profession has the reputation for being one of the unhappiest professions. Or, maybe you associate FEAR, or other fear relatives, (e.g., anger, frustration, hurt, pain, etc.,) with an experience you had with attorneys or other members of the legal community. It is true when fear is present, true happiness can never be achieved. Despite all this, my chapter exists, and I write this completely immersed in happiness energy because I choose how I express myself in my work according to my rules and my integrity. I choose each day to align with who I really am; and as much as possible, I choose love over fear. I am not always successful – at times I fall off the love bus and enter the black hole – FEAR, but my awareness, and knowing I have power - the power to CHOOSE, allows me to re-align with love and access happiness whenever I want.

While studying for the most important exam of my career-the bar exam- the exam that tests on everything a student learned in three years of law school- I embraced the power of acronyms and mnemonics. I used these powers throughout school and continue to use them as I share tools and discoveries as a holistic counselor-at-law and coach.

To me LOVE is: Life's Opportunities to Value Energy while FEAR is simply: False Expectations Appearing Real. Love is eternal and limitless: fear is finite and limiting. I see love as gifts and aspects of our spirits that continue to live beyond the physical. Fear is a burden we carry, an aspect of our bodies, which may terminate (and cease to exist) when we choose or the physical body ceases to exist. Fear is not real. It is an illusion created by our past, our ego and our mind.

As a spirit in a body, living a human experience, we use perception and perspective powers. Perception power is our ability to see, hear, or become aware of something through our senses. We use our senses to value, measure and honor, opportunities around us. After we see opportunities we then label what we see with our perspective power.

Perspective power is the mental view or outlook on something. Our perspective power determines the energy of our experience. The perspective we choose to align with can either empower or dis-empower us. This is determined by evaluating whether the perspective is aligned with our divinity or against it. The perspective we choose to embrace determines whether we are aligned with LOVE energy or FEAR energy.

Perspectives aligned with LOVE energy empower: perspectives aligned with FEAR energy disempower.

Everything is energy. Life offers us the ability to expand and value what we witness and experience. We utilize our perception and perspective powers with each experience, circumstance, awakening, feeling, sight of beauty, or moment of reflection. For the most part, we utilize our perception and perspective powers on a subconscious level. However, being aware and consciously choosing empowering LOVE energy grants you access to happiness energy on demand.

Happiness energy is the mother of all loving energies. It has powers beyond our comprehension and utilization. While many of us in the physical plane equate happiness with material and tangible things, I believe happiness is intangible, immeasurable and has no bounds. I've created the mnemonic: *"Real Happiness Lives Close to the Great House Called Awareness"* (RHLCGHCA). Happiness energy is: **R**esilient, **H**ealing, **L**oving, **C**ontagious, **G**enerous, **H**onest, **C**onnecting and **A**ccepting.

I can recall various times in my life when I did not embrace LOVE energy; and therefore, I was unable to access happiness. During these times I felt powerless and victimized. I felt as though the choices I made were a result of my age, my education, or my life status ("Circumstances") so no matter what my perspective or outlook was about my Circumstances, I was doomed from the start.

I was 28 years old, a law school graduate, and a member of the Connecticut Bar. I was also a temporary employee for the judicial branch making $15 per hour and working as a waitress on the weekends to make ends meet. I lived at home with my parents and was in a long-distance relationship with a man I loved, but couldn't see and enjoy whenever I wanted. I blamed everything on him, on the economy, on my law school, and on anyone (and anything) other than myself. I feared being in that position forever. I feared breaking up with the love of my life because the pain (and hurt) of being so far away might get the best of him or me. I feared having to serve, as a waitress, people I knew, or grew up with, who heard (or knew) I was an attorney. It wasn't until I let my fears go that my life changed for the better. I choose to accept what was real and stopped worrying about what others thought or what might or might not happen. It wasn't real! What was real, was I had choices: I had power, and I chose to no longer give it away.

Happiness, like all energies, is an energy we choose to embrace. Such is the case with fear. When we choose to immerse ourselves in FEAR energy, happiness energy is not readily available to us. In order to access happiness energy, we must choose LOVE energy, rather than fear because the happiness energy is always present wherever love is.

Once I made the decision to embrace LOVE energy, my life began to shift. I knew the FEAR would pass and I'd get all that I needed or desired in life. IT DID and I DO! As I lived with this awareness, I remained in LOVE energy and experienced multiple happiness levels. Happiness energy, as I have enjoyed it, is RHLCGHCA. Again, that is **R**esilient, **H**ealing, **L**oving, **C**ontagious, **G**enerous, **H**onest, **C**onnecting and **A**ccepting.

Resilient: During extreme circumstances happiness holds hope and shares its light. It is resilient. It keeps coming back!

Healing: Happiness holds the ability to alter emotional wounds and physical disease. Allowing, letting go, accepting and choosing better are powerful characteristics of happiness' healing energy.

Loving: Being in a FEAR state while in a happiness state! It's simply not possible! Happiness energy is as limitless as love – there is nothing this energy, feeling, belief, perspective, value or truth cannot DO!

Contagious: Happiness in motion tends to stay in motion – when happiness gets started its momentum is turbo-charged; it can touch, heal, inspire, refresh, and rejuvenate even the most hopeless and depressed.

How contagious is a smile or a friendly hello from a stranger that takes the time to make eye contact with you? How many times do we stare stone-faced or immediately look away from a stranger on the street or in the grocery store instead of exchanging pleasant smiles and hellos? Try extending a friendly smile and hello to strangers you come across during the day. You'll spread happiness energy and reap the rewards from its infectious joy.

Generous: Happiness just keeps on giving! While driving through a Dunkin Donuts drive through one morning, I bought a coffee for the person in the car behind me – just because. If you were the recipient of this gift, wouldn't you feel happiness? Of course you would. I experienced happiness (and excitement) while giving the coffee and while thinking about their response while I drove away. The happiness I experienced while sharing was generous. But the actual giving (and receiving) feeling is an example of, happiness energies' infectious and contagious qualities. I'll never know what the person's response was but I do know that that day I shared my experience with others throughout the morning. The happiness energy was the gift that kept on giving: the coffee recipient, me and those I shared the experience with all felt happiness. Happiness is generosity, an overflowing goodness that shares its light with all who come into contact with it.

Connection: Even enemies that are blessed to share a good laugh can share a moment of happiness. It powerfully connects hearts, lives and experiences. It forges powerful commonalities.

Accepting: Happiness tends to come and go – but it always finds us where we are. It accepts us for where we are. And sometimes it allows us to smile, or laugh, about our strange, or unwitting, circumstances. Being aware of your power to choose happiness is key. Accepting what is and choosing to be HAPPY anyway because you can, is your power.

Is it possible to be 100 percent happy all day, every-day? Well anything is possible. I firmly believe that; however, I think the more probable percentage is in the high 90 percent range because as energy is always moving we are constantly choosing, measuring, and valuing our next steps, actions, and beliefs. Because we are human, I believe we will falter from time-to-time, but due to happiness resilience, we'll keep bouncing back to LOVE and happiness energy again and again!

As an attorney, I am part of a profession that was built around fear and which places limits in an attempt to prevent chaos, all while maintaining order. Even though I am an attorney, and even though YOU may also be a part of (or in a fear-based) an established (or focused) profession or circumstance, LOVE and its entire family is always accessible. With the great awareness of all energies and possibilities, which are unleashed through LOVE energy, happiness energy exists.

The choice will always be there, but you must be aware of your power to make each opportunity your own. Being aware of your power to choose between LOVE- and FEAR-based opportunities you "see" each day, will determine how (and when) you access happiness. When choosing LOVE energy you are choosing your own integrity, your own way, and your own truth. The choice is completely yours to embrace, enjoy, use, and to expand your life experience into anything you intend (or dream) it to be. Choose LOVE and embrace happiness energy. Life is so much easier, magical, and miraculous when lived this way.

ABOUT THE AUTHOR: *SARAH A. OUELLETTE, ESQ.*

Sarah A. Ouellette, Esq. is owner and founder of Response Ability Coaching. Sarah hosts the "Be Happy Summit" which is a virtual online annual event. She is also the creator of the "Live Your Truth and Rock Your Life" coaching program, helping amazing people all over the planet to be bold, authentically real, stretch against the fears that attempt to stop them and live their truth anyway! Because as Sarah says "it's your life, why not go out there and ROCK IT!" Her energy and love for life is infectious she truly believes we all are Rockstars and everyday is a concert of lights, music and crazy fun action.

A pioneer in her field, Sarah is as a Holistic Divorce Mediation Specialist where she incorporates forward focused transition coaching techniques with her mediation legal training and assists families to divorce with purpose, integrity and grace.

Sarah is a Reiki Energy Healer and Soul Re-alignment Practitioner. She utilizes various healing modalities to assist her clients to release blocks and restrictions in their energy fields while allowing space for her clients to intimately learn answers to powerful questions such as: Who am I? Why am I here? What are my gifts? And how can I serve while having the best time imaginable? Sarah is passionate about our divine power to choose and sharing empowering tools to assist us to create the life we dream about. Not every couple she works with breaks-up. Why? When you take the time to look within and fix your Sh*@, you can open up and receive all the ways people want to love you!

Sarah lives in San Diego, California with the love of her life – the man she was dating when she was 27 years old. Sarah and Jonathan met in law school in 2005. They have been dating for nine years and have plans to marry. Sarah enjoys being around the water and sharing life's beauty with Jonathan and their sweet mini labradoodle "Lulu." Her life is a screaming example that miracles do happen. Sarah authentically practices the empowering tools she teaches daily.

You can learn more about Sarah, her work or the Be Happy Summit by visiting her website at: www.responseabilitycoaching.com or contact her directly by e-mail: sarah@responseabilitycoaching.com.

Chapter 11

Orgasmic Happiness

By Dr. Shelly Persad

What is happiness? I used to think I was happy – I lived a very blessed life that never ceased to put a smile on my face. Everyone I knew commented that I was the happiest person they knew… but did I really know true happiness?

Today, I'm happier than ever – I have the dream body, dream husband, dream marriage, dream sex life, dream job, dream pet, dream house, dream life, and even my dream beach house that I've always wanted from the time I was a little girl. I have to stop and wonder, "If this is happiness NOW, what does my future entail?"

Before I share with you how I became so daggone happy, let me share my past with you.

I became a gym rat at the age of 13, and what began as a hobby turned into an addiction that motivated me to compete in figure and fitness competitions to see how far I could take my body. Yes, the perfectionist in me wanted to see if it was possible to obtain my version of the perfect body. This obsession with the perfect body consumed my life – I sacrificed my mental, emotional, social, and physical health for seven trophies that I recently threw out in the garbage. For what? A slice of happiness when I stepped on stage and received adoration from the judges and audience? Was it worth the mad dieting, unhealthy fluctuations in weight, three hours spent in the gym each day, massive amounts of judgment projected at my body in the mirror every morning, bouts of overeating attacks, horrendous acne, hair loss, unbalanced hormones, blown adrenals, lack of social life, and inability to have children?

My mom considered me to be anti-relationship as I swore off anything that even resembled commitment. Besides, I thought that men wanted to hold me back and prevent me from spreading my wings and flying around the world. But don't get me wrong – just because I didn't do relationships doesn't mean that I wasn't getting my needs met. I did sex like a man, literally. I didn't need their number nor did I become emotionally attached after one night in the sack. My peers throughout college often joked that I had a new flavor every week. Was I really anti-relationship, or was I looking for something that I couldn't visualize or verbalize?

I engulfed myself in launching my career as a chiropractor and thought that if I could just make enough money and pay off my student loans, then I'd be happy. I got burnt out working 80 hours per week and fighting insurance companies to get paid, so I ventured across the Atlantic Ocean to Portugal, where I bought an existing practice and hoped that a different culture without the American healthcare system would finally give me the sense of joy in my career that I was longing for. Fortunately, as you'll read here soon, this opportunity didn't work out as planned and shed light on what I was really yearning for.

Throughout chiropractic school and beyond, I attended every self-help and spiritual workshop I could get my hands on. I was also known as a seminar junkie, you know, where you feel really good for the weekend, yet dread returning to your real life.

As you can tell, I've always been a seeker of what else is possible. From the time I was young, there was this deep knowing inside of me that there's more to life than what the eye can see. Yet I misidentified that and was looking outside of my being for happiness – I was hoping to obtain it with my body, food, fitness competitions, career, money, relationships, sex, and even spirituality. The perfect body, countless number of trophies, decent amount of money, multiple relationships and sex partners, and the next spiritual class was not giving me that sense of peace that I now have.

You see, the society we live in today perpetrates this desire for external fulfillment, when really, fulfillment lies within us.

I came to the realization one day that my life is absolutely perfect and the answer to happiness exists right between my two ears and my two legs.

Let me introduce you to sexual energy – I believe this is the most powerful healing force known to man – and it resides right within your very own body. I was introduced to sexual energy through a chiropractic approach that awakened this beast inside of me and facilitated full-body orgasms on the adjustment table, along with deep core healing.

It wasn't until I met my husband, Kumar, and he asked me why I wasn't having these earth-shattering orgasms in the bedroom, that the Universe tapped me over the head with the awareness of what I had been seeking. It was this sexual energy.

All living bodies have sexual energy present in them, however in most people it is lying dormant. You get glimpses of it around the time of orgasm, thanks to nervous stimulation and physical excitation, but then it goes back to being dormant.

When your sexual energy is lying dormant, you're not fully living. Life is robotic – you wake up and go through the same daily routines, day in and day out. This is just going through the motions to have a mundane existence. There is little, if any, awareness and presence in your life.

On the other hand, if your sexual energy is alive and flowing, life truly becomes orgasmic. Everything from your daily routine to work to exercising becomes full of joy and pleasure. Your interactions with others are more pleasant. You always have a smile on your face, and truly mean it instead of using it to cover up the lies that so many of us hide behind. (You know, those people who claim to be happy, put on a smile just because they can, and tell people that life is amazing when deep down they wish they could change at least one thing in their life, not including their underwear.)

So why aren't more people aware of this energy?

Well, let me ask you – how aware are you of the sexual energy that resides within your body?

Often times, we've stifled this energy due to belief systems, programming, and inhibitions around our sexuality. In today's westernized, and highly domesticated, society, we have disconnected from the treasure chest of knowledge on the importance of sexual energy and devalued pleasure, happiness, joy, orgasmic bliss, and sexual ecstasy.

In ancient Eastern traditions, be it Taoism or Hinduism, sex was viewed in an entirely different context. Rather than being the ultimate sin, sexual energy was considered an important pathway to connect intimately with the divine. The divine being a state of wholeness and completeness where you acknowledge the abundance that is implicit in all of us and long for nothing.

Taoists have been exploring human potential in relation to sexuality for thousands of years. The legendary Yellow Emperor recorded conversations on varying sexual matters, providing a great deal of knowledge on ways to use sexual energy to achieve vibrant health of the mind, body, and spirit, as well as longevity, a spiritual connection, nurturing relationships, and optimal pregnancy/birth.

So we may be repressed sexually, but those repressed sexual thoughts, feelings, desires, and urges never disappear; they physically manifest as health issues (especially in the sexual organs), excess weight, anger, frustration, jealousy, addictions to food, drugs, alcohol, reality TV, shopping, gambling, porn, social media, work and power, eating disorders, unhappiness, feelings of unworthiness, judgment, blockages, and lack of abundance, creativity, confidence and wealth. Sexual energy is so powerful that if neglected, the neural pathways that regulate sexuality send messages to the brain that create hormonal reactions that in turn can lead to depression and higher rates of injury and heart disease.

The U.S. government seems to ignore that fact by creating more laws regulating sexual behavior than all of the European countries combined. However, some strange law and $1.5 billion spent on abstinence programs by Congress surely isn't stopping our nation from being sexual – we have the highest teen birth rate in the world, as well as soaring sexual abuse, rape, and porn addiction rates.

Sexual energy is a potent force, however, if used improperly, can result in unwanted consequences. Just like water is a necessity in life, if a water hose is left on, it can create destruction. Sex itself is not the issue; it's the repression of our inherent life force expression. If you don't allow your true sexual self to come out to play, it will come out in other forms.

Have you ever wondered why sex sells?

Sexuality has ties to biological, emotional, physical, and spiritual needs. If any of these needs are not being met, then the "sex appeal" in advertising seduces you under the guise that it will give you exactly what you're missing in life. For a brief moment, that void feels fulfilled, but once the excitement wears off, you're ready to consume the next product that comes along and seduces you.

This influences an egotistic drive within the consumer leading to habits such as cultural acceptance, external gratification, and competing with the Jones'. The by-products of consumerism are impulsive financial expenditure, skyrocketing credit card debt, material possessions associated with survival of the fittest, and the urge to fill a void.

What if the void that sex used in advertising is targeted at is actually your sexual energy? There's a reason sex is the magical formula that persuades consumers to buy on demand. What we avoid becomes a void that we seek to fill.

Look around you – how many people are truly happy?

I don't know many. Despite the amount of money they have or the quality of lifestyle they're living, deep down, people are unbearably miserable.

We don't have to look far:

• 97% of women think negatively about their body daily

- 46% of women struggle reaching orgasm

- 87% of women are sexually unsatisfied

- 52% of couples are unsatisfied with their sex life

- 48% of couples are uncomfortable discussing their sex life

- 67% of marriages end in divorce

- 65% of all U.S. divorces are initiated by women

I've read this following statement multiple times by respected experts, "If there's anything to take away from sex statistics, is that regardless of where you may fit in any of these statistics, you're normal."

Is normal enough for you? Why has it become normal to be a statistic? If we continue on with this mentality, our future generations will not know happiness.

What can we do to attain the happiness we're all seeking?

Well, for starters we can embody our sexuality by enjoying the body we have, choosing more fulfilling relationships, and reconstructing the way we approach sex.

1. Eckhart Tolle once said that transformation is

through the body, not away from it. Through religion, sex education, and the constant inundation of wrongness associated with the body in media, the body has become a sin... something that must be covered up and definitely not a source of pleasure or enlightenment. But wait, if that's the case, then why was the female body designed with an organ, the clitoris, that only has one purpose, and that purpose being pleasure? It's sad that 29 percent of women are unable to locate the clitoris on a diagram.

Sexual energy inhabits our body, but if we don't know our body nor do we love our body, then we are inherently distancing ourselves from this life force energy.

There are two times in your life when you are truly connected to source: orgasm and laughter with total abandon. – OSHO

When you're enjoying a hearty belly laugh or reaching the big O, your mind shuts off and your brainwaves slow to that of a deep meditation. Both instances involve the body – they do not occur outside of the body, which is what we often associate enlightenment with.

In order to fully enjoy the body we have, we must eliminate all judgment related to the body.

2. We have increasing divorce rates due to a few reasons...

First, we often expect our lover to fulfill a hole within us. For example, if you don't know or love your body, then how can you expect your lover to know and love your body?

Second, we're living in an overly masculinized society where both men and women are fighting for power, under the guise of equal rights. In order for women to want to fight for equal rights, they of necessity give up their value of being a woman and view femininity as an inferior class.

As a result, men are becoming less masculine, losing sight of the passion that once ignited them, having difficulty making decisions, and struggling to connect with women. Women are becoming less feminine, losing their intuitive wisdom, escaping in their career, and hardening to the softness and sensuality of life.

Granted, forcing men and women into roles isn't necessary, but two masculine energies cannot be in a relationship for long before they start butting heads and end up sexless. This is where the saying, "opposites attract", comes from – both masculine and feminine energy need to be present in a relationship to create a sexual arc of polarity, thus creating attraction.

And third, we've given up any form of staying power. Once life gets hard, we give up instead of being aware of what's require to change the situation. We choose the easy way out, despite the amount of consequences it may have.

To be in more fulfilling relationships, we must first be in a fulfilling relationship with our self.

3. Whether or not you can reach orgasm does not mean that you are tuned in to your sexual energy. Unfortunately, the way we do sex is very conventional, but it's all we've been taught. I call it the 'wham bam thank ya ma'am' approach. Most people force their orgasm into existence by contracting their muscles, halting their breathing, and expelling the energy outside of their body. This often leaves women feeling frustrated over time and men rolling over to fall asleep.

The alternative would be to relax and surrender to the orgasm, continue to breathe and visualize the energy of the orgasm moving all throughout your body. This not only allows you to harness sexual energy, but it also energizes and revitalizes your body.

Women can learn how to prolong their orgasms, become multi-orgasmic, ejaculate, and tap into their body's capacity to have 13 different types of orgasms. Men can learn how to delay ejaculation, prolong their orgasms, separate ejaculation from orgasm, and become multi-orgasmic as well.

Embodying your sexuality has benefits that are rooted

in your biology. There are three chemicals that have rewarding effects on your life when sexual energy is thriving.

1. Dopamine is a chemical that is part of the pleasure/reward center of the brain – it's present at the time of arousal and when you get what you want sexually. It has been shown to be a source of focus, motivation, leadership, confidence, and decision making.

2. Opioids/endorphins are released at the time of orgasm and have been correlated with terms such as bliss and euphoria. These are the happy, feel good chemicals.

3. Oxytocin, also known as the love drug, is a hormone that creates feelings of bonding, trust, attachment, and connection. Researchers even refer to oxytoxin as the leading chemical of happiness. Oxytocin has also been proven to reduce cravings and addictions, have a calming effect, lower stress, and increase sexual receptivity.

Sexual energy is the energy that brings life to the world and can bring a new life to you when you learn how to channel the energy.

In embodying my sexual energy:

- I have increased self-love for my body, I work out 80 percent less and indulge in the finer things in life, yet maintain a fit and healthy body effortlessly… and I'm happy with my body!

- I magnetized the perfect life partner for me… and I'm happy with him!

- I have mind-blowing hour-long orgasms that cleanse my mind, body, and spirit… and I'm happy with them!

- I have an unbelievable sex life with one partner who can fulfill my every sexual need, want, and desire, instead of being on the hunt for multiple partners… and I'm happy with it!

- I embrace my feminine energy which keeps me attracted to my husband who I allow to be in his masculine energy… and I'm happy being feminine!

- I become irresistible to my husband which makes him desire me and love me more every single day… and I'm happy with him desiring me!

- My heart has opened wider than I ever thought possible, and for the first time in my life I can experience, give, and receive unconditional love… and I'm happy!

So earlier, I mentioned that happiness lies between your ears and your legs, and hopefully by now you've realized that I alone am responsible for my happiness and tapping into my sexual energy has opened the gateway to me being happier than I have ever been.

ABOUT THE AUTHOR: *DR. SHELLY PERSAD*

Dr. Shelly Persad, the founder of Orgasmical Medicine, is a world-renowned orgasmicologist, sexual fitness trainer, author, and speaker. Orgasmical Medicine is a blend of ancient wisdom and techniques with modern day science and research that helps people obtain their ideal body, relationship, and sex life. Dr. Shelly teaches people how to harness sexual energy, the most powerful healing force known to man, and use it to transform all areas of their life.

Her educational background consists of studies in chiropractic, personal training, Ayurvedic Medicine, quantum physics, psychology, tantra and human sexuality. She was a certified global facilitator for a worldwide organization offering empowerment workshops in over 30 different countries. Over the past seven years, Dr. Shelly has facilitated thousands of women on body image issues, relationship difficulties, how to be feminine, and sexual dysfunction.

Dr. Shelly is passionate about sexual health and wellness due to the fact that it is one of the most overlooked aspects of life, yet one of the most important.

Dr. Shelly has been featured on CBS, as well as numerous radio shows, popular online blogs, and in interviews for published books. She is currently the author of several e-books and is in the process of publishing her first book of a series of books on body image, relationships, and sexuality in 2015.

Orgasmical Medicine is much more complex than advocating an orgasm as a cure; it is advocating YOU as a cure. Sexual energy resides inside of you and is the gateway to vibrant health of the mind, body, and spirit, as well as longevity, a spiritual connection, nurturing relationships, optimal pregnancy/birth, and of course, happiness.

When not traveling, writing, or teaching workshops, Dr. Shelly enjoys sharing every waking moment of her life with her handsome husband, Kumar. He is her rock, sounding board, creativity initiator, sexual energy facilitator, the dynamic force who stands beside her, and her #1 fan! Together, they show up in the world to demonstrate to others the living example of all that can be possible in the realm of sex, love, intimacy, and relationships.

Chapter 12

Happiness IS Homecoming

By Josie Blaine

"Most people are about as happy as they make up their minds to be." -- Abraham Lincoln

In many cases, that is true. I asked the nuts lady at my local grocery store, Barb, what makes her happy. She actually manages the bulk section. She isn't certifiably nuts.

"Oh honey," Barb said. "I'm so happy with my memories. I'm so happy with my grandchildren. I think about them, and I get happy."

Barb shared with me that her happiness was derived from times in her life when she shared occasions with those whom she loved most. A very pretty woman and a grandmother, Barb exudes happiness in all directions.

It is clear that she soaked up decades of birthdays, graduations, weddings, anniversaries, and happy occasions, planning to enjoy them again through the gift of memory. Her happiness vibe touches anyone within range and you can't help but carry it with you when you leave the store.

Happy Birthday

One day, on my way home from work, my phone rang. It was my friend Becky.
"Do you still have that menu from your birthday party that year?"

I knew what she was talking about. The year I turned 10, my mom threw me a French birthday party. There was a pink ballerina cake, a dress-up fashion show, and a French menu before dinner. We could each choose two items on the menu, and when Mom translated into English, it turned out that most of my birthday party guests had chosen a napkin and a chair, or a fork and cup. Becky was the only one of my friends who had selected an edible item off of the French menu!

Believing my mom threw the most creative birthday parties, and hoping some of that creativity had trickled down into my veins, Becky enlisted my help in planning her daughter's birthday. After an adventure at the dollar store, during which we decided young Brooke would have a Mardi Gras birthday, complete with lights, beads, bubbles, battery-operated candles on the tables and a French menu, I picked up the phone and called my Mom.

She was tickled pink that her idea from so long ago was still ruminating in someone's mind, and that all it took was a memory of "Le Boeuf" for Becky to create a new happy memory for her little girl. Also, I got invited for burgers.

Parking Lot Party

There we were, a bunch of grown adults, way past graduation day, forced to stand out in the parking lot of our college football dome and tailgate on a bright, sunny, perfectly temperate day, because we no longer qualified for the free student tickets to get into the game. Let's face it, crafting a tailgating site has become almost as big as the game itself, and some of these super fan alumni have artists at the grill now, in their post graduate years. Many tailgaters with sophisticated palettes are not going to settle for nachos with fake cheese (what is that stuff?), and it isn't all that easy to come across game tickets when your team keeps winning national championships.

We stood there, a sea of school colors, in the cool sunshine, with satellite televisions on four sides keeping us apprised of the score. Toddlers dressed as miniature football players and cheerleaders ran to and fro amongst the crowd, in what could only be described as a completely safe environment, if you consider four buses parked in a square, fencing in a crowd of revelers and tables of the best food, and were completely in the moment.

"This," I told my friend Kiel, as we watched kids running and other alumni hugging, "this is a shared experience."

Kiel agreed. The laughter and happiness in the air was energizing. It got me thinking.

Happiness has energy. I mean, what happens when the band strikes up and the cheerleaders run out onto the field or the gym floor? The crowd goes wild! Have you ever seen an angry, bummed-out cheerleader? It doesn't happen! Cheerleaders LEAD the CHEERFUL-NESS! It's their job to bring the happy and the energy to any event!

Why do people go home for Homecoming? Even if you weren't a cheerleader or the president of the student council, there is still a rejuvenation that happens when you reconnect with your core self. Where did your personality begin? Where do you recharge?

Your church group is your shared experience. Your core friends, who get you through thick and thin, are your shared experience, when you don't have to have conversations with full sentences, and everyone laughs hysterically at the inside jokes.

We may all know, or have run across, people who just don't seem happy. A certain amount of energy goes into trying to make them happy, or help them find happiness within themselves. Invite them to positive events. Welcome those individuals along on your journey, but please ensure your happiness fuel tank stays charged. The world needs you and all of your gifts.

Let's say your happiness is a machine, and you need to find an energy source to power this machine. It may be tough for you to keep going to tailgating events, because football season doesn't last all year long. If cleanliness is your energy source, well then, by all means, use all your energy to clean your house and keep everything around you completely hermetically sealed. You might get kind of lonely, because it's hard to maintain a 100 percent anti-bacterial life when you're going out among other people. Other human beings should never be counted on to create happiness. The pressure is too great, and each person is on his or her own journey.

Food as an energy source for Happiness seems to make sense, because from our infancy, our mothers fed us to keep us happy. Food can bring about contentment, but only until the first bite. After that, there had better be something else to replace it.

In my opinion, the best renewable energy resource for happiness is peace. Once you are at peace, you tend to be more forgiving of people. After all, forgiveness is a giving of happiness.

When you are at this level of peace, you will not find the need to eat a large order of fries, but maybe a small or medium. Soon enough, you will be wearing a small or a medium. Order the size food you want to wear! See the correlation? Happiness begets happiness, all around!

Audrey Hepburn told us, "Happy girls are the prettiest."

Mary Lou Retton advised, "Optimism is a happiness magnet. If you stay positive, good things and good people will be drawn to you."

Who can argue with those two ladies? Happiness is a choice. It happens to be a daily choice, so it must be renewed every day, just like showering, to paraphrase Zig Ziglar. I posit to you that the happiest people are the cleanest people.

Consider this: You're on your way to the meeting of your life. This meeting is so important, you bought the 22-pound paper from the resume store, and printed out all of today's necessary documents on it. You took a little extra time with your coif and ensemble this morning, so you stuffed everything into the satchel at your side. You think it is in order. After all, it should be, if it came out of the printer that way.

Walking into your meeting, looking smooth and well-put together, you smile a gleaming smile at the room, take the leather chair at the head of the conference table, reach into your sleek leather satchel that screeches like a record scratch as you cannot find the report you seek.

Happiness and confidence forgot to pack organization and preparation when they left this morning. Whoops.

It's Sunday morning. You're cleaned up in your Sunday Best, sitting in the same pew you've occupied your entire life. For a moment, time stands still while you ponder that. Why don't you ever sit anywhere else? Because this is your family's pew, that's why. Even if you went to another church, somewhere across the country, you'd still sit on the left side, about halfway back, or on the right, in front of the sound booth. It's your familial spot. That pew might be where your parents decided to sit when they married 50 years ago, and they passed this pew on down to you. Someday, if ever the church asks for pew sponsorships, you are totally putting a nameplate on this pew. As the first keys of "How Great Thou Art" begin to play, you rise to your feet, with your family, and think about Grandma, happily approving your ponderances of legacy.

You may not be happy every day. Or, perhaps at the beginning of every day, you have a morning ritual and will begin the day totally revved up, in a state of utter happiness. Then someone collides with your life and will try to run your happiness tank dry. Remember the peaceful renewable resource?

When this happens, take a lesson from our friend Barb, in the grocery store, remember yesterday's happiness. It will get you through today's stress, loneliness and grief. If you ever met her, you would surely think Barb was a cheerleader in another time.

Our brains are such gifts. We were given the ability to choose, and to have memories. If you choose your happy thoughts and memories, you will have more happy thoughts and memories.

And I believe you should make your corner of the world as pleasant and happy as you can, because outside, it won't always be that way. Be safe, be kind, be loving, and as much as possible, create a nice experience for those around you. Surround yourself with precious others, who want to be happy. Be among cherished friends and dear loved ones who smile when they see you. In this way you are assured of more good days than bad. These are the same individuals who will multiply your joy and divide any sorrow that comes your way.

We truly need so little to feel loved and be happy. All we must do is recognize in our hearts the small miracles around us, and be grateful for them.

ABOUT THE AUTHOR: *Josie Blaine*

Josie Blaine's great grandpa worked on the railroad. Generations later, Josie grew up playing on the railroad tracks all summer long in North Dakota. She listened to the trains carry coal all night long. Grandma would keep count of the coal cars, calculating the success of the state.

As most young people did in those days, The North Dakota State University Communications double major hit the interstate, heading south the day after her college graduation. The military kid and radio gypsy has lived in almost every corner of the United States, writing for broadcast, writing for print, and trying out practically every facet of the career of sales/marketing/communications major should. She had a cat. When the cat died, she bought a house and got a dog.

Understanding that mom was right, and there truly is no place like home, Josie sold her house and followed the railroad back to North Dakota. Here, she could write about her own glowing histories, the rumbling trains across the fresh prairies, and her beloved North Dakota, at the side of Grandma's rocking chair.

These days, Josie reports to Grandma on the number of oil cars passing just outside the nursing home, on the tracks that brought the family here so long ago.

Josie loves God, her family, America, The Bison, and coffee. She is the author of the books *Something About Sophia* and *Nowhere, Everywhere.* She appears in local publications.

(Photo by Crown of Laurels Photography, Bismarck, ND)

Chapter 13

How to Increase your Happiness by Heeding the Universal Yes and NO

By Evelyn Fassett

The energy of Yes

Through my own journey I have come to love and respect the path of "following the energy". It also can be described as listening for the energy of Yes.

What is the Universal Yes and NO?

Each of us is provided with an inner compass. If we are careful to keep it in good shape and well used, it will be a tool that can be used by a greater power than we are. I think of it like an antenna. If you are familiar with how an antenna looks, it will have different pieces of metal with different lengths. Each of those lengths is specifically chosen to receive signals of a certain frequency. Our body/minds are like antennae and when we tune in to listen to the frequencies that we are calibrated to receive, that can be used to send us signals that can help guide us. We can feel this as an inner sense, a "feeling", or a more distinct message depending on how we are tuned. This is a gift we all have and it can be strengthened by use.

We can receive the sense that decisions we are about to make are a YES or NO. I like to look at large decisions as a series of smaller decisions linked together. We can practice listening to the messages we receive for all of those varied small decisions.

Intuition – are you listening?

How do I hear it? Does being present matter?

One of the important factors in receiving these messages is *being present*. We may hear a lot about being present and being in the "now". That concept is becoming more widely understood. You may have heard terms like that and wondered how can we be anywhere but in the present moment! Well, there are many things that can keep us from being focused in the present. Many of us are aware of how often we find ourselves drifting to different parts of our life. We might spend a lot of time ruminating about experiences in our past. We might often spend time in the future worried about something that might or might not happen. We could even be living much of our time in an experience that is fairly recent. Perhaps we are stuck in a fight we had with a loved one, a relationship that ended, or a job we have. One of the things that we need to be aware of is that when we are lost in other times and places, then there is less of us available in the present. We receive those universal yesses and nos in the present. Spend your time in the present, actively listening – and you will find it easier to receive the messages. Your mind/body antennae will be calibrated and focused in the right direction for the best signal.

How do I heed it? How do I follow the energy?

The messages we receive are not always clear and to the point. We might not hear the words "Joe! you need to become a doctor, that is your purpose". We are more apt to receive smaller bits of guidance. We might have an opportunity to go to a workshop, or take a class, or start attending a school. We might feel a strong YES about going to that workshop. When I get those pieces of guidance, I will trust them and go. One workshop by itself probably won't make a huge change in your life. It might, however, bring you in contact with the person, or piece of information that will then guide you to another small step. If you consistently listen and then act on those small bits of guidance, you will find that they chain together and create the journey that is your life. Along that path, you will begin to feel your purpose, and will see how they are all linked together and are important. If we try to talk ourselves out of a YES that we receive for whatever reason, (too much money, too scary, too hard, doesn't make sense, etc.) we are making an important choice in that moment. We are choosing to say NO to the Universal YES. The Universe is very loving and non-judgmental and will not necessarily punish us, or show us directly that we made the wrong choice. It will often give us many more little chances to say YES to things that will guide us towards the ultimate goal. So don't beat yourself up for times in the pass that you did not listen or heed. Just notice what your life may have been like if you HAD been listening. Make the choice to start NOW listening and heeding.

What does that have to do with my purpose?

We are all being guided towards learning certain lessons and experiencing sacred contracts with other people that we meet. When you start feeling the flow and wonder that is available to you when you are listening, it is really fun and inspiring.

Start watching for the next YES you get, listen to it and watch what happens. I call it "Follow the Energy". When you have a small decision to make – such as "do I take a class" or not, feel where the yes direction is. If it is toward the class, take one step in that direction. Perhaps make a phone call inquiring about it, or do some research about the subject. Look at how the energy feels at this new point. See if it feels like a door is opening. Maybe when you call the organizer you learn something that you really wanted to learn, or there is some synchronicity – maybe you know the person who answered the phone, or you learn that someone you have wanted to meet will be there. See how easy the flow feels to sign up. If it seems easy and you sense "wow that feels good", take another step in that direction. If it feels like a bunch of blocks are there, notice that. Maybe the website doesn't work, or you can't get hold of anyone. Perhaps the class sounds less interesting after learning more about it. Ask the question out loud- "Is this a no?". Listen and watch for the answer, trusting that it will come. If so, back away and start being observant about the next possible yes coming your way. There will always be many yesses and nos coming your way.

I have heard people comment when something they really want seems very difficult; "We are being tested to see if we really want this." My experience is contrary to that idea. I believe that the Universe makes YES feel open, and NO feel closed. If we keep pushing into a NO with the story that "I need to be doing this regardless of the NO" stop and try and learn where that story came from. Where in your life were you taught that things should be hard. Can we let go of that?

It doesn't mean that our ego won't confuse us sometimes and we will convince ourselves that a NO is really a YES because we WANT it. And we might ignore a YES because our ego or rational mind doesn't think it is logical.

One of the biggest signs that we are in the flow, some call it our Soul Path, is that we notice synchronistic events happening more and more. The more synchronicities we experience, the more we can feel sure we are listening and are in the correct flow.

It takes a lot of energy for the universe to create synchronicities. I live my life watching for them. It is such fun to see and experience them. An example that comes to mind is last summer when I went to a women's conference. I heard the organizer speak and at the time I felt a "YES" about attending. As I learned more about it, I found out the organizer lived in the same town as one of my clients. I had a potential of introducing them. While at the conference, I was able to meet my virtual client in person. We had a wonderful evening together. Also, while at that event, I met several people that gave me little bits of information and guidance that I needed to hear. One day when I was listening to the energy and wondering why I was there, I felt an inspiration to create a group for intuitive networkers. Shortly after receiving that idea, I wanted to go over to a nearby market for lunch. I looked up at an escalator and saw two women coming down. I heard them mention the market. So I walked up and said "Are you going to the market?" Do you know the best way to get there?" They kindly invited me to go with them. While there and sharing our experiences about the conference, I told them about my networking idea. They looked at me with surprise and said that one of them was an intuitive networker and wanted to be included. What are the odds of those things all happening one after another? I could not have made that happen any easier if I had scripted it!

Experiences like that happen to me on a regular basis. I love them, respect them and express gratitude to the guidance that created them. Imagine the energy needed to put both of us in the right place at the right time. I don't feel that I was guided to go to this confer-ence just for that meeting – but once I listened to the YES to go – I put myself in the place where many of these synchronistic meetings could happen and they did. That is the fun of it. Keep yourself OPEN to who you are going to meet, what you are going to learn, etc. When I go anywhere, I keep my antennae scanning for people I'm meant to meet, information I'm meant to learn, etc. It makes everything I do more fun and meaningful. It also gives me more courage to speak to new people because I trust that they might be just the person I'm supposed to meet.

How will following the energy help me?

When you are feeling that synchronicities are happening more often in your life, you experience life less like walls are blocking you, and more like doors are opening for you. You have the opportunity to open your heart with love and gratitude, knowing that you are loved and cared for by something much bigger than you can see. This experience will then help you feel more trust about life in general. When you trust that you will be guided to people you should meet, places you should be and experiences you should have, your peace of mind increases. A life filled with trust and peace of mind is like a well-oiled machine that feeds on itself. The more you feel this way and are listening, the more validations and cool experiences you will have.

Here's the process:

1. Be as much as you can in the Present Moment.

2. Listen for YES and NO when you are making even small choices.

3. Heed the message by taking small steps and testing the energy again.

4. Watch for synchronicities. Move toward whatever causes them to increase and away from what causes them to fade.

5. Feel the love and care that is being bestowed on you.

6. Express Gratitude (the highest vibration emotion there is).

7. Have fun! Be filled with wonder and watch your journey unfold. Feel your peace of mind and trust grow and expand.

8. Repeat again and again!

ABOUT THE AUTHOR: *EVELYN FASSETT*

Evelyn Fassett teaches how to listen to the Universal yes and tune into the energy of the universe. Evelyn has made her own journey from a Software Engineer to Archetypal Consultant, to massage therapist, to Technical Support specialist for creative entrepreneurs. Along that path, she has learned the value of paying attention to synchronicity and the Universal Yes and No. Listen how you can create more Peace of Mind and Trust in your life by doing the same!

Chapter 14

The Art of Creating Happiness After Divorce

By Denise Dominguez

Where do I start? I've pondered this time and time again. I'm going to start at the end because it was my new beginning. I'm going to start in North Carolina. I moved here for the second time in 2012 after leaving my husband again, and for the final time. I was so excited to be here and start my life over again. I picked up right where I left off.

I chose NC mainly because my best friend of 32 years lives here, and her sister does too. For my daughter and myself, the transition wouldn't be so difficult. My daughter and I started working right away and put our stories of heartache and heartbreak behind us as much as we could. We left the only state we ever lived in; the only state we ever knew. We left our entire family in Florida, my son, (her brother) my mom and dad, (her grandparents) my sisters, nieces, nephews, and our friends. But we didn't care about that because we were leaving a toxic relationship that as hard as it was for her to leave her dad, it had to be done.

We had each other and that wasn't scary. We talked about what happened all the time. We talked about what the drugs and mental illness did to our family and knew that there was nothing that could change that. It was hard to face these facts and for my daughter it was sometimes overwhelming and depressing. She has no contact with her dad. None! He wants nothing to do with her and my son wants nothing to do with me and it's because we chose happiness. We chose to get out of that horrible situation and start a new life and they were going to punish us for wanting a better life. Talking about them was important, though. We would reminisce about good times we had as a family and the laughs we shared but we couldn't ignore the traumas and dysfunction we lived in. It was such therapy for us. We would laugh and we would cry. And sometimes we would laugh and cry at the same time. But we were getting through this little by little. I told her that you've lost your dad almost like a death. Because he wasn't here anymore, he was gone. The drugs and mental illness had taken over and he will never be the same and they will never be a father and daughter again and we will never be a family again. Our family was destroyed and there is nothing we can do about that fact. The only things we can do are move forward and make a new life and learn and grow from our life experiences. And that's exactly what we did.

We came here to North Carolina in May 2012. And before you know it the holidays are upon us. How do you deal with being alone for the holidays for the first time in over 20 years?

How does my daughter deal with going from all four of us celebrating the holidays together to just the two of us? What about the gifts? What about the traditions we had as a family? Well...we weren't alone. We had our extended family with us and we had spent so many holidays together in the past, that it was so familiar to us. We kept our family traditions and continued to use them. And the gifts? Ah that was easy! We spoiled each other with whatever we wanted! We baked and cooked and got involved with the planning of the holidays. I wasn't going to let my daughter have a "different" Thanksgiving or Christmas. Of course we were missing two people, but I made sure it was the same in a new way. One of my traditions is to make a new bread basket for the Thanksgiving table every year. Well...for four people the basket was always small. But for this year we had four families celebrating together, so I made a huge basket.

It was the little things that made a difference. It was

our choice to make the first holiday season a sad or happy one. It just didn't make sense to sit around and think about what could have been. It was the better choice for us to embrace the new in our lives and make the best of it! And I know that this is my journey and this is where I'm supposed to be. Yes, I miss having a husband, and yes, I miss my family being all together even in the worst of times, but I will never get that back it's gone. I have to move forward and make new memories and show my daughter what a mom does in tough situations and show her that we are strong and better with the way we are right now! No more yelling, screaming, slamming doors! No more feeling anxiety when her dad walks in the door not knowing what kind of mood he is going to be in. That WAS our life and although we had to sacrifice a lot to leave it we did it! We are making it on our own our journey continues every day and it takes time and we learn about ourselves more and more every day.

Dating Again

My husband was only the third person I had even been intimate with. And what a sexual chemistry we had!!! It was like fireworks every time! Now I'm out there and dating for the first time in over 20 years. How awkward is that? Everything has changed. We are living in a world of Internet and our smart phones are sticking to our fingertips. People don't even look up when they walk. So where do you meet people?

How do you find a date? Not the way I remember it! Usually it was at work or through friends but now... I'm making a dating profile and writing a brief description of who I am. But who am I?
I just got out of a 20 year (toxic) marriage. I was broken and I didn't even know it.

My very first date was with a guy that was not that attractive by the eye. But he was funny and I like that in a man. So we meet for lunch near the hospital that I worked at and looking back wow! It was so awkward. Eating in front of a stranger and trying to talk and see if this person is someone you think you can connect with. I was clueless! I was clueless about the dating world; I was clueless about how to attract the right man for me just clueless!!

Well...he didn't text me every day and I thought that was wrong (because I had no idea how this dating thing goes) so I stopped talking to him. Again, clueless. I was learning pretty quickly that I was attracting the exact same guy as my ex in a different body and oh hell no!!!

So I would take breaks from dating or just talk and text but not really meet them. I was missing the attention of a man but didn't what a man. I was learning about myself, about why I married the man I married and more importantly why I stayed in that marriage for so long. I realized that I was scared! I was scared of him; I was scared of being on my own financially with two small children. I had not had a job in many years, and times had changed. There are software programs that I had no clue of how to use which made me feel even more insignificant and inferior. All of these things had run through my mind for years and years. But when I came time to "buck up" and leave; none of those things mattered anymore. My attitude changed and I went into "survival mode" I knew I had to do this and whatever it took I was going to do it. And I did! It's truly amazing what the mind can do when you have your heart set on something and you go for it. Even when obstacles stand in your way you continue to move forward and get to the point of what you want so badly. You all of a sudden stand tall, shoulders back and chin up. Your body language reflects what your mind is thinking.

The thing was…I was happy! I was happy without a husband, I was happy with my son in another state. My daughter and I lived in a small two bedroom apartment and we LOVED it! It was ours! Our home was finally a safe haven; it was where we could come to and lay our heads down and sleep with no worries of what was next or think about what had happen that day. When we moved in we had a futon couch and air mattresses to sleep on. I decorated it as best as I could and the main thing I wanted on the wall, the thing I wanted my daughter and I to see every time we walked in to our home is a black plaque with a lifted flower print shape of a house mounted on it and at the bottom of the black plaque it says…happy at home. It is so simply, so beautiful and so meaningful. I want you the reader to take these keys points away from this chapter. Never give up! No matter what happens keep going. Never accept less than what you truly deserve. Always have Love in your heart and always, always Love yourself.

ABOUT THE AUTHOR: *DENISE DOMINGUEZ*

Originally from South Florida, where she raised her two children, Denise Dominguez is a coach mentor who helps women by having then face their fears and limiting beliefs that are holding them back.

Denise has a clear vision for seeing the trouble-spots that exist in every "stuck" situation and the creativity to transform it instantly.

She is the creator of the Heartache to Happiness summit for extraordinary women who want to live a "kick-ass" life. Through her own struggles and divorce Denise has managed to come out of it with a smiling face and a positive attitude through it all.

Denise's current mission is completing her book titled: *Don't Let the Blonde Hair and Pink Nails Fool Ya.* Tag line: *I'm smarter and tougher than you think.*

When Denise is not coaching women she is enjoying family time, cooking, traveling and going to rock concerts.

From Denise : As always, I would like to say "Thank You" first! My wish is for the universe to know how incredibly thankful I am for what and who I have in my life. My daughter Sam, who is my biggest fan and supporter! Her wisdom amazes me every day. I am so blessed to have such an intelligent, sensitive, driven and just pure good hearted kid. What did I do to deserve her? It's important to me for you to know how grateful I am for everything and everybody I have in my life. So thank you!!

Learn more about Denise at http://www.denisedominguez.com and join the fun and wisdom at https://www.facebook/pages/denise-dominguez.

Chapter 15

Energize, Visualize, Materialize, Harmonize and Actualize Happiness

By Dr. Aymee Coget, Ph.D.

Level One - Energize

If you are in semi to good shape, stand up, put one hand toward the ceiling and jump up five times while exclaiming "I am Happy!" each time you jump. I am serious, if you want to feel the energy of happiness, go ahead, jump up, exclaim I am happy!

You will feel effervescent bliss in your whole body.

Bliss is one energy of happiness.

Are you smiling?

I recommend doing that throughout the day when you feel the need for a happiness boost

Contentment is another energy of happiness.

Take a deep breath, close your eyes, put your hand on your heart and one on your belly.

Take another deep breath.

Focus your attention in the area of your heart.

Focus on creating an all loving, all nurturing, all accepting open environment in your heart center like you are holding a child at your chest. If that visual is challenging think about the last time you went to the airport to pick up a loved one.

As you create this sacred silent heart space, allow your heart been to come through your chest to the palm of your hand.

When you can feel your heart beat ask your heart to show you what gives you meaning in purpose in life and wait for a response.

Wait patiently for a vision in your mind's eye.

Anything else? Wait for a response. Repeat until your heart is complete.

Then ask your heart "Show me a picture of my true self" and wait for a vision to appear in your mind's eye.

Anything else? Wait for a response and repeat until your heart is complete.

Then ask your heart "What are my strengths?" Wait for a response. Ask anything else? and repeat until your heart is complete.

What you are doing with this inquiry is taking a moment to quiet your mind, and ask your heart the deepest questions that guide your life toward the pond of tranquility.

When you become aware of your heart's deepest MAPS

- Meaning

- Authenticity

- Purpose

- Strengths

and actualize them in your everyday experience you have cultivated the energy of contentment.

You may experience a calm serenity through this exercise, yet this is just a seed of eudaimonia. When fully expressed, this energy is fulfillment in your heart, love as strong as an ox, tranquil as a magic pond and your mind becomes at peace.

Contentment and Bliss are the two most advanced Energies of Happiness.

Before you can truly develop lasting contentment and frequent states of bliss, I first recommend focusing on the first three energies of happiness.

• Empowerment

• Positive Mood

• Resiliency

To cultivate any energy of happiness what so ever you first need to become happy. You can do this by choosing to be happy right now!

I use a declaration written by the Happiness Club Founder Lionel Ketchian.

*I, _____ <fill in your name>do solemnly decide
to adopt the happiness decision
by being happy now!
Rather than react to my problems*

I will respond with happiness
forsaking all negative thoughts
In all ways, I will
choose happiness
for the rest of my life!

Making this declaration has helped many people feel greater empowerment over their happiness when committing to this everyday. It has helped Lionel sustain his happiness for over 20 years!

The next energy of happiness is positive mood.

I recommend instituting a positive mood boosting routine throughout your day. This includes activities like smiling, laughing, reminiscing over positive memories, expressing gratitude, kindness, exercise, and healthy eating habits. Other happiness skills that create a positive mood are positive thinking, using positive language (eliminating no, not, don't, should, but, try), and present moment awareness.

If you are one to experience a higher ratio of negative thoughts over positive this is a skill that will keep happiness energy away from you.

If you are allowing your mind to wander half of each day, you are drifting away from your happiness energy.

Energy of resilience is the other essential ingredient for your sustainable happiness.

This will help you swim instead of sink in the face of adversity. If you let the energy of the world overcome your energy of happiness suffering will ensue.

When challenges come up in your life respond with happiness as you declared in your happiness decision.

Level Two - Visualize

Empowerment

Imagine being the band leader, the quarter back, the governmental leader, the traffic director, the airline controller. IMAGINE BEING SUPER MAN OR SUPERWOMAN. Feel the power of being in charge and invincible. Feel the power of knowing what to do and when to do it. Feel the lightness as you inspire those around you and the strength you feel inside with confidence of knowing where to go and what to do.

Positive Mood

A sunny day. Morning Sun on your face. A gourmet cup of your favorite coffee with the exact right amount of cream and sugar. A home made warm chocolate chip cookie. An enthusiastic jog in the park among rare trees and flowers. Candy. Chocolate. A smile from a stranger. A new dress. New shoes. New electronic device. A raise. Recognition of a job well done. A celebration of a prized event. Togetherness with your loved ones or those who share the same values. A day at the beach. A long nature walk. A beautiful Sunset. A good night's rest.

Resiliency

Bouncing back after adversity. Feeling you overcame the challenge. You triumphed. You fought hard, thought you were unable to make it and POW! You come out on top! You gained stamina and perseverance to get your body in shape after you felt fat. You learned beauty was on the inside after a terrible bout of cystic acne. You learned to love yourself when your dream man/woman was someone other than you thought. You learned to separate how your mind from your body when your body is compromised in pain. You learn how to overcome learning disabilities and naysayers. You learn the power of post traumatic stress disorder and how to manage forgiveness of the worst of human sins. You learn how to have compassion in the face of hatred. You learn how to know your true self when others judge you. You learn your worth is beyond your bank account. You learn realistic optimism and know this to shall pass as progress in your self development for the rainbow only comes after the rain.

Contentment

This is a peaceful fulfillment in your deepest heart of hearts. Meaning in life is circulating in your veins. Purpose pulsates through your heart. Your authentic self is raw, real, and actualized. Your strengths are your God's gifts naturally flowing every day. You feel full inside knowing you are making a difference in the world. You see recognition in others and in the world from your commitment to your truth. You feel a constant presence. You feel strong, willing to accept your path, even if it seems challenging or even hopeless for you know you will never be content unless you are able to truly find your heart's greatest calling. You know your heart's voice is different than your ego and you trust your inner guidance to lead you in the right direction. There is an absence of questioning, wondering, or pontificating. There is only right action, peace, serenity, tranquility, and calm. An inner strength in your heart as strong as an Ox and peaceful as a white dove, serene as a tranquil pond.

Bliss

Nirvana. Euphoria. Ecstasy. Enlightenment. Awakening. Joy. Lightness. Faith. Oneness. Imagine being connected with all there is. Imagine a oneness, a lightness, a refreshed and rejuvenating feeling. You are doing yoga. In meditation. In worship at church. A synagogue. An ashram. A mosque. Or a natural setting. Your eyes are rolling back in your head, there is an effervescence inside, a dissolving of a human experience meaning there is an absence of thoughts, emotions, or physical sensations. This is a place, a feeling, or a state of constant connectedness with the Divine or feeling part of something greater than yourself. Bliss is a bi product of a frequent state of positive mood, deep contentment or a connection to something greater. This lightness effervescence is strong, peaceful in nature and bright like the north star.

Level three - Materialize

Years of studying, teaching, writing, critiquing, interviewing, meditating, and applying the concepts led me to an incredible humility as I have learned from great teachers and synthesized all I was taught in a five-step process model. If you are inspired by others who have developed this prized sustainable happiness you can apply the model to your own life.

Standing on the shoulders of Giants

ODE TO JINENDRA SWAMI - MESSENGER OF SUSTAINABLE HAPPINESS.

I have studied sustainable happiness with Jinendra Swami since 2003. He has taught me a variety of important lessons including: You can only help others become happier if you are happy. One key of living in the now is to forget the previous moment. Create your life based on the simple question: "Does this make me happy?"

Structure of Gratitude - I am grateful for ___ because it adds ___ to my life. Focusing on the life contribution strengthens our deepest sense of gratitude. Humming changes your brain chemistry. Negativity in close relationships breeds absence of universal harmony. How to be everywhere, any time. When all else fails, jump up and say 'I am happy!' Thank you Jinendra for your spiritual guidance over all these years. I feel blessed to have you in my life.

Ode to Dr. Bob Nozik, retired physician, esteemed academic and extravagant contrarian eccentric.

My wise man on top of the hill is an unassuming Jolly Old Man who overcame the hedonic treadmill of goal achievement and landed himself in over 20 years of sustainable happiness. Dr Bob entered my life in 2003 and became my mentor in all areas of life; personal, love, family, academic, and professional. I based my Happiness Makeover™ on his keys to happiness: conscious awareness, present moment living, self like/self love, self esteem, handling mistakes, acceptance, non judgment, appreciation/gratitude, individuality, optimism, and perfectionism. Before Dr. Bob entered my life, I was unaware of your inner critic. I had developed my positivity so strongly, I never knew most people had to fight the battle every day inside of their head with most peoples worst critic: ourselves. Creating a system to counter, train, and transform your inner critic to your inner colleague is one of the most crucial skills of sustainable happiness. With a deep inner critic, sustainable happiness is impossible. Dr. Bob also showed me the power of living in the moment. His book inspired me to live in the now which I have been doing since 2006. After six months of active training, it finally stuck and my stress decreased, productivity increased, flow and ease in life began. Dr. Bob taught me two of the greatest sustainable happiness tools: a process to shift negative thinking to positive thinking and present moment awareness. Dr. Bob also taught me about the happy idiot syndrome and appropriate happiness. Your guidance in my life has kept me on my happy track through thick and thin.

Ode to Lionel Ketchian - Founder of Happiness Clubs World Wide

Lionel developed a sustainable happiness beyond 20 years based on the simple commitment to choose happiness above all. He taught me the power of empowerment over our own happiness. Generously sharing his happiness, teaching others and communicating with those worldwide on how you can be happy has inspired me day in and day out as I help spread the empowerment through this words in pledge of the happiness decision.

Ode to Dr. Robert Mueller - Former Secretary General of United Nations/ Nobel Peace Nominee/ Author

Dr. Mueller was in his 80s when we met in 2005. I interned with him learning about his life and his keys to happiness. An incredibly inspiring man who is no longer with us on Earth, he taught me crucial lessons including the power of intention, how to have the happiest day every day, how to commit to world peace and do whatever it takes to leave a positive foot print. Thank you Dr. Mueller for helping me see the power of intention as we clearly set it day in and day out.

The next levels are to harmonize, and to actualize happiness. As you traverse your path of developing sustainable happiness, I invite you to experience, visualize, and materialize in order to harmonize your world with your own inner voice as it will guide you to states of elation, euphoria and eudaimonia.

Peace be with you.

ABOUT THE AUTHOR: *DR. AYMEE COGET, PH.D.*

Dr. Aymee Coget (Pronounced Co-jay) is a thought leader and teacher in the field of sustainable happiness. She has been on a mission to help millions of people live happier lives since 1996.

She has an international consulting practice based in San Francisco, CA. She has created multiple positive psychology and leadership courses which have helped people recover from suicide, depression, anxiety, and stress so they can feel healthier and happier than ever before in their lives.

She has consulted with major global corporations, mainstream media, governmental groups, and gives speeches on the topics of sustainable happiness and positive psychology to enhance well being and reduce stress.

She has written a book called, *Sustainable Happiness in 5 Steps*. Her Ph.D. is in organizational psychology with an emphasis in feminine authentic leadership and positive psychology.

Chapter 16

30 Days Sugar Free

By Barry Friedman

I was programmed for what happiness was supposed to taste like since I was a baby. Two of the first three ingredients in my baby formula were different names for sugar. When it came time for solid food, I would spit up anything that wasn't sweet enough to satisfy my finely tuned baby-palate.

As a toddler I was bribed, rewarded, and punished with varying amounts and forms of sugar. "You've been such a good boy," my mom would announce, "let's go get an ice cream!" I can still picture the disapproving look on my father's face when he would say, "that was a very bad thing to do - no dessert!"

Like many of you, I was placed on the sugary path that has led this culture to rising levels of concern including cardiovascular disease, obesity, high blood pressure, skin issues, tooth decay, and depression. Children today are a part of the first generation in history who are expected to live a shorter life than their parents.

And you want to talk about happiness? You have the opportunity to turn the train around!

It was February 28, 2012 when my nine-year old son and I were enjoying a big cup of frozen yogurt with all the toppings. Mini peanut butter cups, gummy worms, hot caramel sauce, and probably a few more that my mind is sparing me from having to recall. After making sure to scrape out every last bit of the goodness, we loaded into the car and he asked the question, "Daddy, what are you going to leap for Leap Day?"

The concoction wrestling in my stomach answered for me. "Sugar, Zed. I'm going to leap sugar for the day."

Silence, followed by, "I'm not going to join you on that, but how about if I don't pick my nose for the day?" We all have our battles.

I don't know what date you are reading this, but I can tell you one thing for sure. Figure out the amount of time between right now and Leap Day 2012 and that is how long I have been sugar free.

How can I be so cocky? How can you trust that I am still sugar free? Here's the deal: would you ever buy a ticket and wait in line to see a movie that you hated the first time? Right, me neither.

I woke up on March 1st, 2012 feeling like a million bucks. Empowered, rested, stronger, younger, and exactly like that guy who was able leap tall buildings in a single bound! Before even getting out of bed I turned to my wife and told her I was going to do 30 days sugar free! Knowing me and my sweet tooth for more than half of my life, she asked what exactly I planned on eating. I wasn't sure, but I knew that was a detail I could work out.

Where is the happiness in living life free of all pro-cessed and refined sugar? So glad you asked! Let me summarize a few of the areas that have been most impacted for me personally, and then I'll share some of the stories from people around the world whom I have coached through 30 Days Sugar Free.

Internal Changes

Sleep

Sleep, oh dear, precious sleep, where have you been all my life? Were you kept at bay because of all the junk that my body was forced to process all night long? Did the amount of sugar I ate each and every day make it all but impossible for you to take over my mind and body and carry me into a restful slumber?

My unconscious late night snacking usually included ice cream, chocolate, or some other form of sugar. These foods raised my blood sugar and delayed sleep. Later, when blood sugar dropped too low (hypoglycemia), I would wake up and be unable to fall back asleep.

Deep sleep has freed up my time and opened the door to possibilities I never imagined. I now function at 100 percent on six hours of deep sleep whereas my sugar-filled self could barely wake up and force a smile after eight hours in bed.

Colds/Flu

For me, it always started with that little ping in the throat. It was like seeing a number in my Caller ID that I dreaded, but knew was coming. The next few hours were always the same: lots of water, some Chinese herbal medicine that a friend swore 'would knock it out before I even knew I had it', and some western medicine just for good measures. I'd make sure to get to bed extra early and picture myself waking up all better.

Never worked. Not even once. I was the Elvis Presley of colds - the King. When it landed on me I was signed up for seven to 10 days of bottom-of-the-barrel existence. I lost my voice from extreme soreness, had pain throughout my body from exhaustion, and coughed up phlegm that looked like what people used to smoke in the 1980s. Very unpleasant and very predictable.

In my time since going sugar free, I haven't spent a single day with a cold or flu. Those 21 - 30 days of my life each year are mine again - to love, play, travel, write, connect, and thrive. That is a very real, very tangible piece of happiness that I will never give back nor take for granted.

Anxiety

Joni Mitchell said all there is to say about this one, "Don't it always seem to go that you don't know what you got till it's gone..." Such has been my experience with anxiety and sugar. I can, if I squint and let my mind drift backward, recall the racetrack that was my mind and body when I ate sugar. Obsessively counting anything and everything, running what/if scripts over and over, shallow breathing, fidgeting with my fingers or feet - all of this and more and I never realized I was doing it.

After my first month sugar free, when the chemical, physical, mental, emotional, and social habits of sugar were gone from my life, I realized that I was, probably for the first time in my life, present. In fact, as I sit here writing this, I take a deep breath and feel wetness in my eyes. I feel a mixture of sadness and joy from all that was and all that is.

My ability to hold conversations or meditate, focus on a project or completely relax, speak on stage or look into my son's eyes - none of that was pure or easy before getting the toxicity of processed and refined sugar out of my blood stream. Happiness is a very real energy that has blossomed thanks to a seemingly simple, yet counter-intuitive change I made on Leap Day, 2012.

External Changes

Weight Loss

The only reason many people would ever consider something as radical as 30 Days Sugar Free is to lose weight. Seriously, on first examination, this challenge has the sex appeal of learning Morse code, memorizing Pi, or playing the oboe. Yet for those who have tried and failed at the art of reducing their physical girth, this has been a life-changing experience. Be it the commitment, the support, the black-and-white boundaries – it works.

I was never what I'd call huge. I'm 6'1" and at my heaviest I wore a size 36" waist pants, and weighed

in at 189 pounds. As of this writing I am still 6'1",
well, of course, and I'm back at my high school pant
size of 32" waist and tilting the scale at 165 pounds.
That's a lot of Reese's Peanut Butter Cups, Snickers,
and cookies – and honestly, I can't imagine what it
would be like to eat any of that again. Those calls
have been permanently transferred to an unchecked
voicemail box. The sweet tooth has fallen out. And
I'm one svelte 52-year old dude!

Skin

I recently saw some video of myself from 2008. After
coming out of shock, I called my wife in from the
other room. She heard the panic in my voice and came
running. I didn't even need to say anything – she saw
the TV screen, looked at me, and came and sat by
me. Puffy. Wrinkly. Bags under my eyes. Pockmarks.
Heavy eyelids. Dead.

This was a testimonial video that I made for a book
review and I can't imagine anyone even heard the
words I was saying. Surely it was all masked by their
disbelief that a man who looks like this would have
the nerve to appear on screen!

Looking like that snuck up on me. Clearly I was fine
with how I looked back in 2008 because I shot a lot
of videos. We age gradually and most changes aren't
noticeable day to day. Looking back at that video,

however, I now look look 10 years younger than I did in 2008 – and that has been confirmed by a woman who has known me since 1986 and confesses, "This is NOT the body I married!"

Happiness Changes

Mindset

Kicking a lifelong habit to the curb gave me more than just internal and external changes. It handed me the super power of knowing that I can do anything imaginable.

Picture this: you remove something from your life that is making you sick, fat, tired, and unhealthy - and something that has, on some level, been making your insides unhappy for a very long time.

What messages might that one change send to your psyche?

• I care about myself

• I put my health first

• I find ways to reward and celebrate myself that promote my health

• I model the power of choice to my friends and family

- I live as the healthiest version of myself

- I can change any habit I have

- I don't wait for governments or administrations to take care of me

- I laugh at what others think is impossible

- I nourish myself because I am valuable to my loved ones and the world

- I don't rate my enjoyment based on how much sugar I eat

Is it really important that our psyche receive positive, uplifting, and happy messages? Those messages are ground zero for a cycle that determines everything in your life. Your thoughts influence your feelings which affect your actions and determine your results.

This flow has been happening since you were a baby, and it's immutable. Everything begins with the thoughts. Happy thoughts yield happy results.

Since quitting sugar I created a hugely successful, global coaching program to support people in going 30 Days Sugar Free. The 10 bullet points above made it impossible for me to contain my verve for the topic, and my results have touched lives around the world. I have appeared on over a dozen television shows talking about a sugar free lifestyle, written a book on the topic, and offer expert interviews to media outlets including blogs, newspapers, and other authors around the world.

Changing my diet gave me new messages (thoughts) that influenced my feelings which affected my actions and determined my results. B I N G O !

And because I have the aforementioned superpower, I can now hear you saying, "sure Barry can do it, he's _____." I'm leaving that line blank so you can fill in your own reason for why I can do it and you can't. I've heard enough to know that we're all different when it comes to projections! But, I believe you can do this. And I have been helping people do this for several years now, successfully.

When I hear from people whose lives have changed, this has been a powerful experience for me. As a parting shot I'll invite you to consider the connection between what you eat and how that supports who and how you aim to be in the world. Just like any organism, our fuel source determines so much in terms of how we function. I've found the sweet life that lies beyond the addiction to processed and refined sugar, and would support you in a 30-day visit, anytime.

ABOUT THE AUTHOR: *BARRY FRIEDMAN*

I could easily have been voted "Least Likely Person to Ever Go Off Sugar for Single Day" before this whole crazy idea came to me on Feb 28th, 2012.

As the taller and balderhalf of the comedy and juggling show the "Raspyni Brothers," I have won two World Juggling Championships, performed on over 100 national television shows, and appeared live over 2,500 corporate events for Fortune 500 companies since 1982. Literally thousands of domestic and international opportunities to eat really sugary treats.

I give my time to this site for one reason: to support anyone that wants or needs to go 30 Days Sugar Free. I am all in, 100 percent, for anyone that is willing to put some consciousness and intention around what they eat for 30 days.

There's a saying: if you don't decide what you want to do with your life someone else will. It's my experience that the same goes for your mouth. My tagline around this project is: Own Your Mouth for a Month. It really sums up what I believe happens when you make a choice like this.

My dear friend of over 20-years, Michele Rothstein, and I both quit sugar within a few days of each other. The odds of that happening, when we hadn't spoken to each other in over six months, were so small that I figured we just had to run with it. I have been married to my brilliant and talented wife, Annie, since April of 1988. She writes extensively about parenting, teaches music to young children, and is an awesome homeschool mom to our son. She's never had my addiction to sugar. I dream about being able to have her relationship to sugar – very healthy and moderate.

My son once went 30-days without sugar in exchange for a laptop. This was way before I quit and I'll never forget how impressed I was with his willpower – at birthday parties, after dinner, or out to eat. Then again, he has been my greatest teacher since 2002. I know that him seeing me do this is having a profound effect on his understanding of possibility – and I trust that will serve him well in the future. You can find more at www.30DaysSugarFree.com.

Chapter 17

A Happiness Recipe

How to use meditation, gratitude and laughter to cure pain and produce joy in our life

By Maria Kellis

I like to think of life a little bit like I think of cooking a good meal in the kitchen that I would prepare for my family, or for those special friends that are also my family. So let me talk about a recipe for transmuting the pain in our life through meditation, gratitude and laughter into happiness and joy.

I remember hearing as a child that it is when the night is darkest that is the time when the light of the new day is about to shine. So I wanted to test this as a child. I remember staying up all night waiting for the sunrise to come. I loved watching the stars shine. Most often I would end up falling asleep waiting for the sunrise. Sometimes though, I would manage to stay awake and I noticed that there was a moment when it felt very cold, even in the summer. It was a moment when the night became still and that moment was always right before the first light of dawn came into the sky. It is a circle that repeats every day. Every day those rays of sunlight hit the horizon. As many come together, eventually they light up the sky. It is in those darkest moments of the night that those rays of sun always appear.

I like to think of gratitude and of laughter as the first rays of sunshine that come somewhere in the horizon and illuminate that absolute darkness of the deepest and coldest part of our hearts. I am going to talk about the light. I am going to talk about how to get in touch with those first rays of sunshine that hit the horizon and about how to bring light into the deepest night.

Let me tell you a story about how I learned to use gratitude and laughter to cure pain. Pain of the physical kind, real pain, the pain that a few painkillers would not take away because it is pain of the very soul that becomes physical pain. And the energy of gratitude and of laughter is the energy that brought me relief, a solution and a cure.

I had to understand that gratitude and laughter are the

power that brings joy. I see now just how incredible that power is, because I know the process of where the laughter comes from, and where it is that the joy leads us. I imagine that I am a kid again, that I am in the middle of the night and I trust that when it is in those darkest moments that the new light of dawn will come. Gratitude brings laughter, laughter brings joy and joy brings happiness. Laughter is the first ray of sunshine that lights my path towards the light.

My process began with my introduction to meditation. This process started to come into my life many years ago. At the time I had a life full of accidents, pain, and hospital visits. It was for me a time of real darkness, of absolute absence of light. Nothing seemed to penetrate that thick veil of cold in my heart. I felt despair because it seemed that tomorrow would never come, or if it did come it would be so terrible, maybe it would be better if it never came. Now I know that in the circle of life this is the moment before the new dawn comes, these are the moments when life becomes still because next comes the light that will shine so bright.

I came from the world of figures, numbers, proofs and exactness. I was an engineer trained at the best schools. I was a lover of math and numbers and I knew beyond the shadow of a doubt that one plus one equals two and there was no explanation needed or flexibility in between. So, it was by accident that I discovered meditation. I had my life planned perfectly and I thought that everything was in the right path. In fact I assumed that until I was really old with a great fortune and grandchildren I would not have to change anything in my perfect life. I assumed I knew it all and I would never need anything to change. I was having what they told me was a perfect life. Why would I want anything to be different? I was following all the rules by the book, being a "good student" of life. So it came as a terrible surprise when everything was turned upside down.

It seemed to me that it was really bad luck that left me paralyzed in the hospital and in so much pain there were no painkillers that really could work for me. And it was at the hospital, after many weeks of recovery, because the pain was so terrible and relentless, that really out of desperation the doctors gave me a tape for meditation. The tape was so old that it was a real cassette tape and I had to ask someone to buy a tape player so I could play it. In this tape I had to imagine pain as fire, and water that I would extinguish the fire, the pain. I tried it out of desperation and to my surprise I realized that it was working. This was the first time meditation came into my life.

Through meditation everything became peaceful and quiet. I was in a different place, I was happy. I was so happy I felt that I felt that I was floating on air many times. I experienced this joy that love brings us when we join with spirit. I understood the absolute and powerful joy of spirit and my life could never be the same again. I spent many years meditating. I was going up and down and somehow life was never the same. There is an indescribable happiness on the other side. I remember this time so many years ago when I meditated for the first time and that experience made me want to keep meditating forever.

I was riding the wave of life again. And as time passed I forgot the intensity of my desire to be in that joy, in that bliss forever. Certainly I was meditating but I was little by little getting back to the day to day events of life. Yet life always reminds us what we forget. Nature is very kind to us. If we forget our spirit's true purpose, it is at that moment that spirit reminds us to go back. In a way as the wheel of karma turns we are able to go from darkness to light again.

The first ingredient that came to me for this recipe for a life of happiness is meditation, a nice regular meditation practice. And as I was meditating I learned that there are other benefits to meditation, except the obvious first one of reducing pain. This is a recipe for pain management though, so the first ingredient to remember is meditation.

So maybe one more day passed in the karma life because I had, unbelievable as it may seem, another terrible occurrence. This time it was a near death experience. The actual crossing over was again a reminder of how amazing the other side is, how much love and joy exist in spirit. The actual details are a story for another time. The ingredients in my recipe that I want to tell you about are gratitude and laughter and how they brought me healing in my life.

I did come back to life, and when I came back again I was in terrible pain again, because my body was broken. I knew my lesson of meditation from the last time but this time I had more to learn. Let me tell you how it happened that this new time I was given the secret of gratitude and of laughter.

My mother came to the hospital to be with me. I was in so much pain I could not move and I was not in the mood for much. Yet my mother was determined to make me laugh, so she started making jokes. She would create a joke out of every story and she would make it so ridiculous at one point I could not help it, I started laughing. She seriously would take everything and make it funny simply by repeating it or noticing the little things that are out of place or unusual and then she would exaggerate them. In fact we brought so much energy of laughter that all the people around us – I was in a room with six patients and their families – and even the nurses, we all started laughing with my mom. Something incredible happened then. My pain went away. I did not quite understand it but the laughter brought me relief and joy.

I had many weeks of intense pain ahead of me so I got to practice a lot. There were moments when the pain was so intense there was nothing I could do. Yet I learned the game. I would laugh and as I was laughing it was as if a blanket that would come over me and take the pain away. I started to learn to laugh at the silliest things. My mom was my ally and we could laugh for hours over nothing. Laughter was the strongest medicine I could give my body. Yet, my mother was not always around so we can laugh together and so I had to really think of a game that would allow me to stop the pain on my own. I did make a mental note for the future to surround myself with these special people that really can make me laugh though.

Over time again I have found a few more tricks to making my life a life of laughter. I remember the times in the hospital and my mother with her endless silly jokes. I noticed that some people have this magical ability to laugh and I realized that what we laughed about were the silly things that we shared. I notice those people and I keep them close to me. I also realized for the times I am on my own that I can make lists of silly things I could laugh about. Now I notice that spontaneously I laugh about things and I laugh in pure joy. The magic comes from pure joy. I notice the little things of life, the little things that are so simple and uncomplicated. When I laugh it is healing not just for my body, it is healing for just about everything in my life. And now I am the one who makes others laugh around me. This is how the ingredient of laughter came into my life for this recipe.

Gratitude I had heard is the key to unlocking the secret of love. Over time I invented a game for myself during those months of recovery. I was stuck in bed hoping that I would eventually get better. The game was the cure of pain through gratitude. I would start with a list. A list of things I was grateful for. I was making a list of what I was grateful for. I would always start the list with "I am grateful because my eyebrows do not hurt" this was always true in those long months of recovery. So I would start by saying these words and continuing to the next thing I would be grateful for. "I am grateful that I am wearing clothes." "I am grateful that I have a clean bed." I was in pain, so the first few items on my list were always the hardest to come up with, because I was not able to think and since I was in pain I was not really grateful. Yet as an exercise I would list one item then I would come up with another item and little by little my list was getting longer and longer. And as the list was getting in the 150 items, this was the magic number for me, I would feel so much gratitude that I would simply forget that I was in pain, in fact the pain would go away, and instead I would feel joy in my heart, strength in my body and happiness became who I was.

I have found over time that gratitude is a very easy and powerful way to shift my mood, my energy.

Saying thank you out of my heart, truly is healing to me and to those around me. And saying thank you to the love that is all around us, flows through us and around us for the things we have is actually the best state of mind to be in, the best way to live. So this was the last ingredient in my recipe for pain management. Gratitude.

I like to talk about the magic of life. I like to talk about the magic of life as a recipe. So here is my recipe for producing joy and happiness when there is pain in our life. We start by having a regular practice of meditation and prayer, maybe five minutes a day as a start. We put gratitude one item at a time. Slowly we start mixing it with laughter. As we mix it all together then we start seeing the mixture produce sparkles of joy. We carefully gather those in our heart and we warm them up with extra love. We keep it in our heart. Over time this mixture produces miracles. And as we experience the miracles we add more gratitude and more laughter. And they occupy our heart space, to the point when there is no more space for anything else and what we thought of as pain simply cannot stay in our lives anymore. The closer we are to that space, the more our life is a life of miracles and the miracles are our life. For best results, repeat daily.

ABOUT THE AUTHOR: *Maria Kellis*

Rev. Maria Kellis is a certified spiritual healer. She has been helping people find out how to strengthen their desires and make their dreams come true. After many accidents, pain and a near death experience, from being a business person and an engineer, she has totally switched gears – she now shares the joy of life - she travels around the world – and she works as a coach for people to connect to their purposes. These days her home base is Bali, Indonesia. She has managed to restore her health, achieved independence and lives a life of freedom.

For all these, she has found a way to achieve effortlessly and enjoyably while still performing in this world at the highest levels. Generating miracles is the answer to life's problems. Money, fame, health, and relationships: The question is not if you can do it, rather how fast can you do it?

Maria Kellis was born In Greece, grew up in France, and went to college in the United States. She holds two degrees from MIT, a degree from the Sloan School of Management and a degree from the Academie of Cannes. She has achieved high honors and high level positions. She achieved a lot in her life as a person of this world. She worked hard and participated in the creation of companies. She was able to get also great jobs – as high as working as an advisor to the Vice President of Greece, and as head of the technical services for the Church of Greece.

Chapter 18

Are you Choosing Pathetic or Powerful? The Gift of Happiness

By Erica Glessing

When happiness is being elusive, reach inside for guidance. Ask for happiness. Ask "what would it take for me to experience happiness in this very moment of time?" Ask and the answers will show up. Then heed the answers of your spirit, for the calling is bigger than you are.

If it were so easy to slip into the mode of happiness, like tuning to a radio station, more people would be experiencing happiness in any given moment. And it is, actually, easy. Yet, the mind plays games and old neural pathways get stubborn, holding on to ways of being that don't bring happiness.

I'm going to for a moment put myself in the shoes of someone who is not happy. And that's difficult because I do wake up happy. I experience happiness most hours of most days. Happiness is my over-arching place of being. The magic of joy and synchronicity happens for me every day.

So I'm going to think about a time when I felt pathetic. And when I say that I felt pathetic, this doesn't mean I actually was ever pathetic. It's just that sometimes it is easier to feel like a pile of poop than a magic, powerful change agent. "Plus if you've been told you were pathetic, or not wonderful, or too much, or too ugly, or too fat, well, you may have bought into a lot of packs of lies that no longer serve you. Are you going to start seeing the brilliance of you? Or will you keep looking at the places where your life feels more like poop?

Because when I think my life is not working, and when I am in this space of not being willing to discover my own beauty, well, unfortunately, I get more of that. And the more I see that things aren't working, the less things work. I call this pathetic, or feeling small, or choosing unhappiness. You can much more easily choose unhappiness than choose happiness, for the most part. Because unhappiness is everywhere. And on the flip side, happiness is everywhere, also. Just because there are more oysters than pearls, would you stop believing pearls exist? Happiness is like that. It's a beautiful pearl and the capacity for it is within you, all the time.

The more I see things as working, the more they work.

The more I see myself as a powerful magician with the ability to bring light, love, joy and brilliance into every dark corner I ever step into, the more joyful I feel. Then I am able to give this place of being to others, and that's when I personally hit extreme joy.

What questions can you ask of yourself today to bring you closer into your light? Here are some questions to ask yourself every morning on your journey into happiness.

"Does this action feel like love or feel like fear?"

"Am I believing I am pathetic or am I believing I am power-ful?"

"Does this choice feel like joy or feel like pain?"

"If I change my perspective, is anything even more amazing possible?"

"What would it take for me to experience happiness today?"

"Where will I be if I make this choice today, in the years to come?"

As you stay focused on joy, love, happiness, and the absolute and firm commitment to experiencing "All is

Well," you will notice your life becoming more full, beautiful, colorful, enjoyable, and you will see the people shift to be near you or to let you be.

Changes into Happiness

When you start knowing that you are not pathetic, and when you firmly see yourself as brilliant and powerful, this will shake up a few people. You may find that you can't be around everyone you used to be around. You may see where others can't see their own light, and stand firmly entrenched in their own confirmation of how much they dislike their lives. I can pretty much bet they were told that they were pathetic by well-meaning teachers and parents who sought to "correct" them. So the reasons and excuses go on for miles, as far as when people choose to stay stuck. Luckily, you don't have to change anyone. Luckily, when you change your own consciousness, everyone around you experiences it and gets closer to the light. If someone isn't ready to accept light, he or she may feel repelled by your new light. So there can be lonely moments when you shift into a new level. Let this be alright, because the next level will bring new people into your lives and then even more alchemy can occur.

One of my dear friends is building a new networking platform, and I'm talking about the kind of platform where people meet each other, not the computer kind.

So he is so bright and brilliant with his global vision, and his energy is so clean and joyful, that it is a complete and total high to be in his space. I love his vision and hearing about his plan to teach others to connect deeply and serve each other. Yet, I am present to the fact that there will be those who reject his brilliance. There will be those who cannot learn how to network the way he teaches it. So should he change and be pathetic so everyone can get him? Or should he stay in his vision and see who joins him?

It's sometimes easier to see the right thing when it isn't about you. When it's about you, and the changes you are supposed to make to be in your brilliance, the rubs begin to show up. The obstacles begin to show up.

Navigating Blocks to Your Happiness

Pay attention to your language. Pay attention to the words you speak, as it will give you clues to how your mind is working. When you choose to see beauty, joy, and exceptional power in every single human being, you will notice that your life changes forever. When you let go of judging yourself and others, your happiness climbs instantly.

One block to your happiness is pretending you are pathetic.

One block to your happiness is pretending you can't be happy.

If anyone on the planet is happy, you can be too.

One block to your happiness is to buy into beliefs that don't fit your soul, psyche and spirit anymore.

Start in this moment, right now, fresh, joyfully, leap across the oceans of self-pathetic words you may have chosen to say about yourself, and stand in the place of extreme joy, happiness, power and magic.

Go with me here, and feel into that space of recognizing the beauty in your life.

My gift to you today is about feeling into the space of your own power. Stand in this with me, go here with me. It feels so different and fresh. And recognize that happy today won't be happy in 20 years. So if you felt happy in a corporate job, and you don't anymore, it is because you have changed. So honor this new place that you are, and trust that all the ways will show up to take you into your next levels of being.

When the quiet voice speaks to you in the morning, and tells you what will bring you happiness on that given day, listen. Heed the calling. And know your power.

ABOUT THE AUTHOR: *Erica Glessing*

Erica Glessing was born into a family of journalists, publishers and printers. She began writing professionally in 1984. She writes original "Happiness Quotations" most days, with more than 1,000 quotations written at the time of this writing. You can find them at www.Facebook.com/HappinessQuotations.

Erica is a gifted writer, editor, third generation publisher, and a psychic medium. Her company, Happy Publishing, is dedicated to publishing works that change the world.

She is happiest on the beach or near the ocean with her family. She is a mom to three beautiful children. She loves four-legged beings as well. Curling up to read by the fireplace after walking on the beach brings her happiness. Plus, inspiring you!

The END

CPSIA information can be obtained
at www.ICGtesting.com
Printed in the USA
LVOW03s2250251117
557582LV00009B/162/P